CONTENTS

INTRODUCTION

This book is designed to cover the course for Bookkeeping – Manual and Computerised at Further Education and Training Awards Council (FETAC) Level 5. Since bookkeeping is a very practical task, this book is designed to explain the process of bookkeeping using practical tasks at each step of the process from source documents to trial balance and bank reconciliation.

Part 1 provides students with the necessary knowledge and techniques in order to operate a manual bookkeeping system. This section presents 34 individual tasks together with detailed explanations on how to carry out each task and the solution to each task. The section concludes with four further exercises, each of which requires the student to repeat all of the tasks.

Part 2 deals with the installation of TASBooks, the creation and setting-up of a company. Each step of the process is explained clearly in a step-by-step manner, including images of the screens as they appear during the process.

Part 3 deals with the computerised bookkeeping method. This book uses TASBooks to explain the computerised process, but the work can easily be applied to any computerised accounting program. This section has 41 tasks, which follow the same sequence as the manual section, and includes the additional topics such as report printing, backup files and restore files. Each task is clearly explained and includes images of the screens as they appear for each task.

This section also includes a transaction summary, which provides a quick reference on how to perform any of the tasks necessary for this course with program references and page references for the details for each task. The section concludes with four further exercises, each of which requires the student to repeat all of the tasks.

Part 4 provides a sample manual project for the FETAC assessment of the module Bookkeeping – Manual and Computerised. This section also includes solutions and a sample detailed marking scheme.

Part 5 provides a sample computerised examination for the FETAC assessment of the module Bookkeeping – Manual and Computerised. This section also includes solutions and a sample detailed marking scheme.

A separate booklet provides all the necessary source documents required to carry out the individual tasks set in the book. This booklet also includes sample, blank daybooks and ledgers that may be photocopied and used with Part 1.

The year digits on all documents have been deliberately substituted with the symbols ## so that the book is not year-specific, thereby allowing the book and source documents to be used for any year.

ACCOUNTING TERMS

Before we begin our work we must firstly understand some basic terms:

1 Source
   Document: All entries made in the company books originate from a
               source document. A source document contains all the data
               relating to a sale, a purchase or any other transaction
               affecting the company. The relevant details from the source
               document are transferred to the appropriate daybook.
                   The most common source documents are:
                       Sales Invoices
                       Sales Credit Notes
                       Purchase Invoices
                       Purchase Credit Notes
                       Customer (Debtor) Receipts (cash or cheques received)
                       Supplier (Creditor) Payments (usually a remittance
                       advice)
                       Petty Cash Vouchers
                       Record of any other payments made (e.g. VAT, salaries,
                       PAYE/PRSI)
                       Record of any other monies received (e.g. dividends,
                       VAT repayment)

2 Daybook: A book, or more commonly, a card or sheet onto which the
              individual daily transactions of a business are written.
              Daybooks will be examined in more detail later.

3 Account: One particular person's or item's details including all
              transactions for that account.

4 Ledger: A book containing all the accounts of a particular type.
              Sales Ledger: This may also be called the Debtors'
                                 Ledger, and contains customers' accounts.
                                 Each account is contained on a separate
                                 card or sheet.
              Purchase Ledger: This may also be called the Creditors'
                                 Ledger, and contains suppliers' accounts.
                                 Each account is contained on a separate
                                 card or sheet.
              Nominal Ledger: This may also be called the General
                                 Ledger, and is where all transactions end
                                 up via various routes. Entries are normally

transferred from the other books or ledgers, but it is also possible to make entries directly into the nominal ledger. Each account in the Nominal ledger is contained on a separate card or sheet.

5 Debit: This is an amount written in the Debit (Dr) column of a daybook or ledger. Some accounts are referred to as 'Debit accounts' because the balance in the account at any particular time will normally be a Debit amount.

6 Credit: This is an amount written in the Credit (Cr) column of a daybook or ledger. Some accounts are referred to as 'Credit accounts' because the balance in the account at any particular time will normally be a Credit amount. One of the most important things to learn is whether an entry in a ledger is a Debit or Credit entry. This will be explained when dealing with ledger entries.

VALUE ADDED TAX (VAT)

This is a tax that is charged on goods and services. This tax is imposed by the government, and VAT-registered businesses are required by law to collect this tax and forward it to the Collector General every month or two months. When a business sells a good or service they add on the appropriate amount of VAT to the cost of the goods or services.

In the operation of any accounts, there are a number of different VAT rates that will be used. It is essential to understand the different VAT rates. In the case of computerised accounting, the computer program keeps track of each VAT rate by using a separate VAT code for each rate and produces a report listing all VAT rates for the purpose of making VAT returns to the Revenue Commissioners.

In the manual system, the Net amount of the goods is recorded at the various VAT rates, and in this way it is possible to calculate the VAT at the various rates.

There are eight different VAT rates in common use at present. These VAT rates are determined by the government and may change from time to time. For this reason there is no attempt made to ensure that the VAT rates used in this book are the ones in use at any particular time. The computer uses a code to reference each of these VAT rates. The VAT rates and the computer codes used are as follows:

CODE	RATE	DESCRIPTION
1	20% Resale	This standard rate applies to goods that are sold or that are purchased for the purpose of selling again and that have a rate of 20% applied to them.
2	12.5% Resale	This is the same as the first rate, but applies to items (usually services) that have a rate of 12.5% applied to them.
3	0% Resale	This rate is the same as the above, but applies to items that have a 0% VAT rate applied to them.
4	Exempt Resale	This only applies to companies that have a Section 13A VAT exemption certificate. This certificate can be obtained by companies that export more than 75% of their produce.
5	20% Non-resale	This rate applies to all goods, having a rate of 20%, that are purchased for use by the company in running their business and that will not be resold.

CODE	RATE	DESCRIPTION
6	12.5% Non-resale	This is the same as the above, but applies to items that have a rate of 12.5% applied to them.
7	0% Non-resale	This is the same as the above, but applies to items that have a rate of 0% VAT rate applied to them.
8	Exempt Non-resale	This rate only applies to companies that have a Section 13A exemption certificate.
9	Outside Scope Rate	Outside the VAT scope. We will not be using this, but it must be set up as it is a default rate.
M	Multiple Rates	The computer program also understands the character M as a VAT Code, and this is used when more than one VAT rate is used when entering a source document, and therefore more than one code is required.

PART 1

Manual Bookkeeping

1 Manual Bookkeeping

In order to run any business efficiently, it is essential to keep proper accounts. A good system for keeping accounts manually has been devised over the years and is well tried and tested. This system is known as the 'Double Entry' system and is used in this book to record the normal transactions in a business on a day-to-day basis. These day-to-day records will then be posted to the necessary ledgers in order to keep the company accounts up to date and to produce a trial balance.

A company will have a number of books into which the data from source documents is entered. These books are referred to as *daybooks, books of first entry* or *books of prime entry*.

The manual accounts system uses the following daybooks and ledgers:

* Daybooks
    Sales/Sales Returns Daybooks
    Purchases/Purchases Returns Daybooks
    Cash Receipts (Bank Lodgement) Book
    Cash (Bank) Payments Book
    Petty Cash Book
    General Journal

* Ledgers
    Sales (Debtors') Ledger
    Purchases (Creditors') Ledger
    Nominal (General) Ledger

The operation of each of these will be examined individually, using examples in each case. A summary diagram of the bookkeeping process is shown on page 4.

It is sometimes difficult to know where to start teaching bookkeeping. Some would suggest that the obvious place to start is with purchasing, as you cannot have a business without firstly buying something. This is a valid argument, but it is difficult to start at this point, as the student has no knowledge of the business at this point.

A more successful point at which to start is with sales. If someone started work in the office of a business, it is most likely that they would be dealing with sales long before they would be dealing with purchases. This allows familiarisation with the type of business, stock items, prices, etc., and allows the student to get to know the running of the business gradually, and in a logical manner.

A computerised accounts system to perform the same work will also be explained, and it will be possible to compare both systems.

Bookkeeping – Summary Diagram

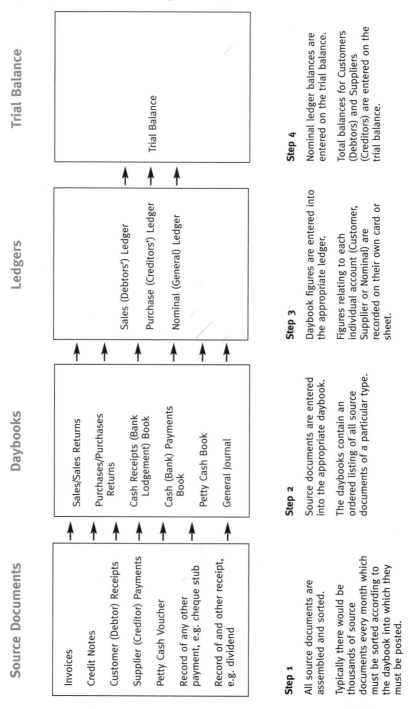

Source Documents

Invoices

Credit Notes

Customer (Debtor) Receipts

Supplier (Creditor) Payments

Petty Cash Voucher

Record of any other payment, e.g. cheque stub

Record of and other receipt, e.g. dividend

Daybooks

Sales/Sales Returns

Purchases/Purchases Returns

Cash Receipts (Bank Lodgement) Book

Cash (Bank) Payments Book

Petty Cash Book

General Journal

Ledgers

Sales (Debtors') Ledger

Purchase (Creditors') Ledger

Nominal (General) Ledger

Trial Balance

Trial Balance

Step 1

All source documents are assembled and sorted.

Typically there would be thousands of source documents every month which must be sorted according to the daybook into which they must be posted.

Step 2

Source documents are entered into the appropriate daybook.

The daybooks contain an ordered listing of all source documents of a particular type.

Step 3

Daybook figures are entered into the appropriate ledger.

Figures relating to each individual account (Customer, Supplier or Nominal) are recorded on their own card or sheet.

Step 4

Nominal ledger balances are entered on the trial balance.

Total balances for Customers (Debtors) and Suppliers (Creditors) are entered on the trial balance.

Source Documents

All entries made in the company books originate with a source document. The relevant details from the source document are entered into the appropriate daybook. It is worth noting at this stage that the work of the bookkeeper is to record the data accurately from the source document and not to change the document if there is an error on it.

The source documents which are used in this book are:

Sales Invoices
Sales Credit Notes
Purchase Invoices
Purchase Credit Notes
Customer (Debtor) Receipts (cash or cheques received)
Supplier (Creditor) Payments (usually a remittance advice or a cheque counterfoil)
Petty Cash Vouchers
Record of any other payments made (e.g. VAT, salaries, PAYE/PRSI)

It is essential to become familiar with source documents and be able to identify the necessary data that needs to be recorded in the relevant daybook. The following is a typical invoice with the relevant data identified. However, invoices differ in shape, size and layout, and students should become familiar with as many kinds of invoices as possible.

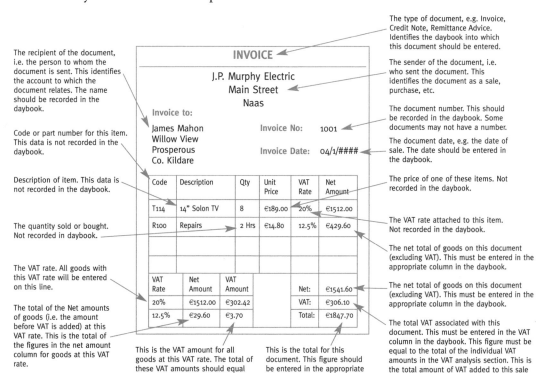

2 Daybooks

Sales/Sales Returns Daybook

The Sales/Sales Returns book is used to record the details from all sales invoices and sales credit notes. This book explains the use of a combined sales/sales returns daybook to record the sales invoices and the sales credit notes (sales returns). Some businesses may use separate books (pages) for the sales and the sales returns, but both systems are in common use.

The source documents for writing up this book are the invoices and credit notes issued by our company, i.e. the company you are working for. Entries in the daybook should be in date order.

We will now commence work with our first task. In order to perform this task you should have a Sales/Sales Return Daybook (Source Documents page 185).

TASK M-1

Enter the Sales Invoice on Source Documents page 3 into the Sales/Sales Returns Daybook.

This task requires you to enter the details from the invoice into the Sales/Sales Returns Daybook.

Every time an invoice or credit note is issued to a customer the data from the document is entered into the Sales/Sales Returns Daybook. This daybook has a number of columns into which entries should be made, as follows:

Date:	The date of the invoice or credit note should be entered in this column. Entries should be in date order.
Customer:	The customer name should be entered in this column.
F:	The F stands for folio, which is used to trace this entry in the company books. The folio here will usually be the initials of the sales ledger (SL) as that is where this posting will appear. The folio is usually inserted when the entry is being posted to the ledger and may also contain a number that references that particular account in the sales ledger. Posting to ledgers will be explained later.

Inv./Cr. Nt. Number:	This column contains the invoice or credit note number as displayed on the invoice or credit note.
Total:	The gross total amount on the invoice/credit note including VAT should be recorded in this column.
Net Amounts:	There may be two, three or more columns used to record the net amount of goods at various VAT rates. These amounts are normally totalled on the invoice, but if not then it is a simple matter of totalling the net amounts at the various VAT rates from each line to the invoice.
VAT Amount:	This column records the total VAT amount as shown on the invoice or credit note.

When you have completed this task, your daybook should look like the following:

COMPANY NAME: J.P. MURPHY ELECTRIC

Sales/Sales Returns Daybook   Month: January ##

Date	Customer	F	Inv./Cr. Nt. Number	Total	Net Amount @ 20%	@ 12.5%	VAT Amount	Analysis Sales	Repairs
06/01/##	James Mahon		1001	453.60	378.00	—	79.38	378.00	—

TASK M-2

Enter the sales invoices on Source Documents pages 4–7 into the Sales/Sales Returns Daybook.

TASK M-3

Enter the sales credit note on Source Documents page 8 into the Sales/Sales Returns Daybook.

The entry of the credit note is the same as the entry of the invoice, with the exception that all the money amounts must be recorded as minus amounts. This is done by placing the amount in brackets or by placing a minus sign in front of each amount. In recording figures, it is very easy to fail to notice a minus in front of a number and therefore it is common practice in accounting to place the amount in brackets to indicate a minus amount.

It is also a good idea to use a different colour for the recording of credit notes, however it should be clearly understood that the colour of the entry has no significance beyond this.

Note:

(i) In the case of credit notes, the amounts are recorded as minus values by placing a minus sign in front of the figure or by placing the figure in brackets.

(ii) The entries in the Sales/Sales Returns Daybook must be posted subsequently to the correct ledger account. The posting of these entries will be explained later.

Completed Sales/Sales Returns Daybook for January after entering transactions:

COMPANY NAME: J.P. MURPHY ELECTRIC

Sales/Sales Returns Daybook   Month: January ##___

Date	Customer	F	Inv./Cr. Nt. Number	Total	Net Amount @ 20%	Net Amount @ 12.5%	VAT Amount	Analysis Sales	Analysis Repairs
06/01/##	James Mahon		1001	453.60	378.00		75.60	378.00	
07/01/##	The Electrical Shop		1002	1847.70	1512.00	29.60	306.10	1512.00	29.60
09/01/##	New Age Contractors		1003	4952.85	4058.00	74.00	820.85	4058.00	74.00
11/01/##	Cash Sale		1004	49.95		44.40	5.55		44.40
12/01/##	Tomorrow's Electronics		1005	4279.50	3483.00	88.80	707.70	3483.00	88.80
13/01/##	New Age Contractors		1006	(549.60)	(458.00)		(91.60)	(458.00)	

Note:

The folio (F) reference (SL in this case) is not usually entered until the figures are transferred to the ledger.

Summary Note

Sales invoices and credit notes are entered in the Sales/Sales Returns Daybook:

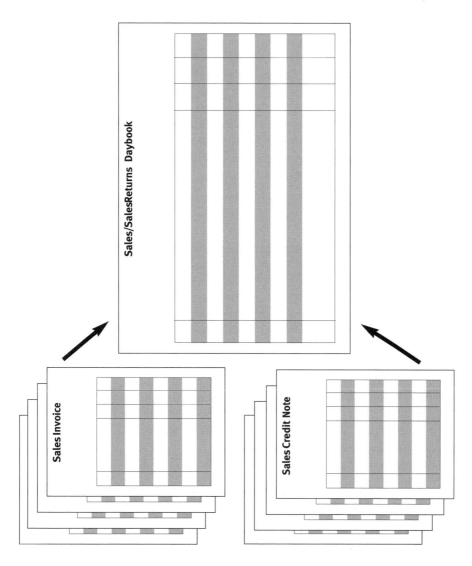

Cash Receipts (Bank Lodgement) Book

In the running of any business, all monies received must be recorded accurately. All monies received, whether cheques or cash, will be lodged to a bank account. These receipts are recorded in the Cash Receipts (Bank Lodgement) Book.

The Cash Receipts (Bank Lodgement) Book is the second daybook that we will be using. All receipts should be recorded separately, with each individual receipt occupying a single line in the Cash Receipts (Bank Lodgement) Book. Since lodgements to the bank are normally done only once per day, all the receipts for that day will have the same lodgement number.

We will now continue our work with the next task. You will require a Cash Receipts (Bank Lodgement) Book (Source Documents page 186) in order to perform this task.

TASK M-4

Enter the receipt of the cash, for the cash sale invoice on Source Documents page 6 into the Cash Receipts (Bank Lodgement) Book. (The lodgement slip number is 101.)

This task requires you to enter the details from the cash sale in the Sales Daybook or the cash sale invoice into the Cash Receipts (Bank Lodgement) Book. There is no source document in this case, as the cash will be received when the sale is made.

The date used for the entry of the cash sale is the date on the invoice as the money is lodged to the bank on the date of sale. In some businesses, where the amount of sales would be very small, there may not be a lodgement every day, and in such cases the lodgement date may be different to the invoice date. Another method of dealing with cash sales is to use a cash till and to lodge the till takings to the bank in a single entry.

The entries in the Cash Receipts (Bank Lodgement) Book are as follows:

Date:	The date of the lodgement should be entered in this column. In the case of cheques received it is the date of the lodgement that should be entered and not the date on the cheque. In the case of cash sales, it is the date of the sale, as the money is received immediately.
Details:	The details of this lodgement, such as the customer's name or cash sale.
Lodge. No.:	The lodgement number for this lodgement. (Remember, when there are a number of items lodged at the same time, they will all have the same lodgement number).

F:	This stands for 'folio', and is the ledger reference for tracing this posting in the company books. The folio will usually be 'SL' (sales ledger), as nearly all monies received will be from customers. The folio is usually inserted when the entry is being posted to the ledger, and may also contain a number that references that particular account in the sales ledger. Posting to ledgers will be explained later.
Bank	The amount lodged to the bank for this entry. This will be the amount of the cheque or cash.

When you have completed this task the Cash Receipts (Bank Lodgement) Book should look like the following:

COMPANY NAME: J.P. MURPHY ELECTRIC							
Cash Receipts (Bank Lodgement) Book					Month: January ##		
Date	Details	Lodge No.	F	Bank	Cash Sales	Debtors	Other
11/01/##	Cash Sale	101		49.95	49.95		

TASK M-5

The cheque on Source Documents page 9 was received from James Mahon and was lodged in the bank on the date of receipt. Enter this lodgement in the Cash Receipts (Bank Lodgement) Book.

This task requires you to enter the details from the cheque into the Cash Receipts (Bank Lodgement) Book. The source document in this case is the cheque from the customer. Since all cheques are lodged on the date of receipt, the lodgement date will be the date of receipt.

TASK M-6

Enter the remaining cheques received on Source Documents pages 9–10 into the Cash Receipts (Bank Lodgement) Book.

Note:

The entries in the Cash Receipts (Bank Lodgement) Book must be posted subsequently to the correct ledger account. The posting of these entries will be explained later.

Completed Cash Receipts (Bank Lodgement) Book for January after entering transactions:

COMPANY NAME: J.P. MURPHY ELECTRIC							
Cash Receipts (Bank Lodgement) Book					Month: January ##		
Date	Details	Lodge No.	F	Bank	Cash Sales	Debtors	Other
11/01/##	Cash Sale	100		49.95	49.95		
12/01/##	James Mahon (chq 204587)	101		453.60		453.60	
21/01/##	The Electrical Shop (chq 215687)	102		1847.70		1847.70	
22/01/##	New Age Contractors (chq 272357)	103		4403.25		4403.25	
25/01/##	Tomorrow's Electronics (chq 467832)	104		4000.00		4000.00	

Note:

The folio (F) reference (SL in this case) is not usually entered until the figures are transferred to the ledger.

Summary Note

Cheques and Cash Received are entered in the Cash Receipts (Bank Lodgement) Book:

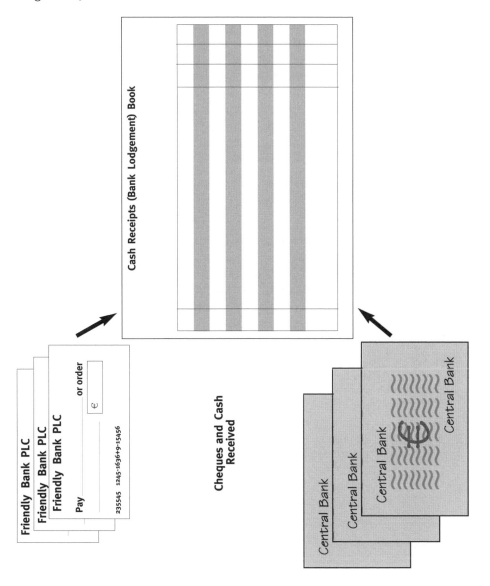

Purchases/Purchases Returns Daybook

The next book that we will be using is the Purchases/Purchases Returns Daybook. In our case we will use a single book (page) for the purchases and the purchases returns. As in the case of sales, some businesses may use separate books (pages) for the purchases and the purchases returns, but again, both systems are in common use.

The source documents for writing up this book are the invoices and credit notes received by our company from suppliers. Entries in the daybook should be in date order.

We will now perform the next task, for which you should have a Purchases/Purchases Return Daybook (Source Documents page 187).

TASK M-7

Enter the purchase invoice on Source Documents page 11 into the Purchases/Purchases Returns Daybook.

This task requires you to enter the details from the invoice into the Purchases/Purchases Returns Daybook.

Every time an invoice or credit note is received from a supplier, the data from the document is entered into the Purchases/Purchases Returns Daybook. This daybook has a number of columns into which entries should be made, as follows:

Date:	The date of the invoice or credit note should be entered in this column. Entries should be in date order.
Supplier:	The supplier name should be entered in this column.
F:	The F stands for folio, which is used to trace this entry in the company books. The folio here will usually be the initials of the purchases ledger (PL), as that is where this posting will appear. The folio is usually inserted when the entry is being posted to the ledger and may also contain a number that references that particular account in the purchases ledger.
Inv./Cr. Nt. Number	This column contains the invoice or credit note number as displayed on the invoice or credit note.
Total:	The gross total amount on the invoice/credit note including VAT should be recorded in this column.
Net Amounts:	Goods that are purchased may be resold later and therefore are categorised as Goods for Resale. Goods for resale may be purchased at more than one VAT rate, and a separate column should be used for each separate VAT rate. In our example, we will only be purchasing goods at one VAT rate, and in this event the net amounts or the goods are entered in the Goods for Resale column. Alternatively, goods may be purchased for use in the running of the business. These goods include electricity, telephone, fixtures

and fittings, etc. These goods are categorised as Goods Not for Resale. Goods not for resale may also be purchased at more than one VAT rate, and a separate column should be used for each separate VAT rate. We will be using only one rate for non-resale, so the net amount of the goods is entered in the Goods Not for Resale column.

There may be two, three or more columns used to record the net amount of goods at various VAT rates. These amounts are normally totalled on the invoice, but if not, then it is a simple matter of totalling the net amounts at the various VAT rates from each line to the invoice.

VAT Amount: There are two VAT columns. One is for recording the VAT amount on Goods for Resale and the other is for recording the VAT on Goods Not for Resale. These columns record the total VAT amount as shown on the invoice or credit note. Some daybooks may only have one VAT column but this makes it very difficult to separate the VAT on goods for resale and VAT on goods not for resale when completing the VAT 3 form.

Analysis: The analysis columns are used to group the purchase of various items into the categories required by the management of the company. The net amount of the goods recorded on the invoice or credit note is then entered in the appropriate analysis column according to its category.

In this example the items are divided into four categories, namely Purchases (Stock), Electricity (Elec.), Telephone (Tel.) and Fixtures and Fittings (Fix. & Fit.). However, there may be any number of analysis columns. The totals of these columns record the amount of expenditure for that particular group and would be recorded in a separate account in the Nominal (General) Ledger as will be explained later.

When you have completed this task, your daybook should look like the following:

COMPANY NAME: J.P. MURPHY ELECTRIC

Purchases/Purchases Returns Daybook   Month: January ##

Date	Supplier	F	Inv./Cr.Nt. Number	Total	Goods for Resale Net@20%	Net@12.5%	Goods N for R Net@20%	VAT Amnt	Purchases	Analysis Elec.	Tel.	Fix. & Fit.
02/01/##	Solon Intl		216457	6336.00	5280.00			1056.00	5280.00			

TASK M-8

Enter the Purchase Invoices on Source Documents pages 12–13 into the
Purchases/Purchases Returns Daybook.

TASK M-9

Enter the Purchase Credit Note on Source Documents page 14 into the
Purchases/Purchases Returns Daybook.

The entry of the credit note is exactly the same as the entry of the invoice
with the exception that all the money amounts must be recorded as minus
amounts. This is done by placing a minus sign in front of each amount or by
placing the amount in brackets. In recording figures it is very easy to fail to
notice a minus in front of a number and therefore it is common practice in
accounting to place the amount in brackets to indicate a minus amount. It is
also a good idea to use a different colour for the recording of credit notes,
however it should be clearly understood that the colour of the entry has no
significance beyond this.

Note:

(i) In the case of Credit Notes, the amounts are recorded as minus values by
placing a minus sign in front of the figure or by placing the figure in
brackets.

(ii) The entries in the Purchases/Purchases Returns Daybook must be
subsequently posted to the correct ledger accounts. The posting of these
entries will be explained later.

Completed Purchases/Purchases Returns Daybook for January after entering transactions:

COMPANY NAME: J.P. MURPHY ELECTRIC

Purchases/Purchases Returns Daybook   Month: January ##

Date	Supplier	F	Inv./Cr.Nt. Number	Total	Goods for Resale Net@20%	Goods for Resale Net@12.5%	Goods N for R Net@20%	VAT Amnt	Analysis Purchases	Analysis Elec.	Analysis Tel.	Analysis Fix. & Fit.
02/01/##	Solon Intl		216457	6336.00	5280.00			1056.00	5280.00			
03/01/##	Philem Irl		78542	2376.00	1980.00			396.00	1980.00			
12/01/##	Mod. Com.			66.90			55.75	11.15			55.75	
13/01/##	Solon Int		5347	(158.40)	(132.00)			(26.40)	(132.00)			

Note:

> The folio (F) reference (PL in this case) is not usually entered until the figures are transferred to the ledger.

Summary Note

Purchase Invoices and Credit Notes are entered in the Purchases/Purchases Returns Daybook

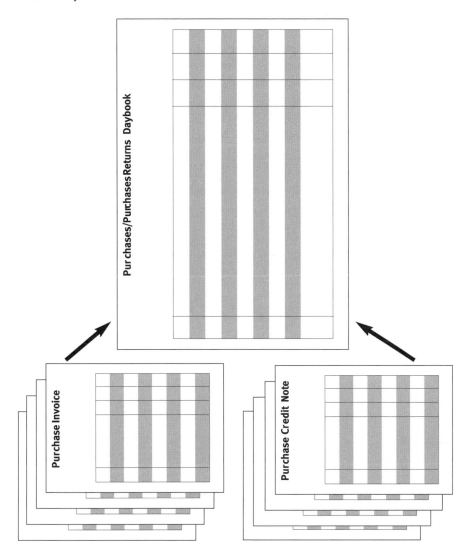

Cash (Bank) Payments Book

In the running of any business, all monies paid out must be recorded accurately. The Cash (Bank) Payments Book is used to record all payments made by the company. Payments are normally made by writing a cheque, by direct debit (DD) or standing order (SO), and drawn on their bank account. Payments to suppliers normally have a remittance advice attached to the cheque, and it is the remittance advice that is used as the source document in this book.

The Cash (Bank) Payments Book is the fourth daybook that we will be using. All payments should be recorded separately, with each individual payment occupying a single line in the Cash (Bank) Payments Book. The number of analysis columns may vary greatly from one business to another depending on the way in which the business wants its payments analysed, but each entry in the daybook will have an amount in at least one analysis column.

We will now continue our work with the next task. You will require a Cash (Bank) Payments Book (Source Documents page 188) in order to perform this task.

TASK M-10

Enter the details from the remittance advice on Source Documents, page 15 into the Cash (Bank) Payments Book.

This task requires you to enter the details from the remittance advice into the Cash (Bank) Payments Book. The source document in this case is the remittance advice that is sent with the cheque to the supplier.

The entries in the Cash (Bank) Payments Book are as follows:

Date:	The date of the Payment should be entered in this column. This is normally the date on the remittance advice or the date of the DD or SO.
Details:	The details of this Payment, such as the suppliers name or what the payment is for (e.g. salaries, rent).
Cheque No.:	The cheque number for this payment. In the case of a direct debit, the letters 'DD' are entered, and in the case of a standing order, the letters 'SO' are entered.
F:	This stands for 'folio' and is the ledger reference for tracing this posting in company books. The folio will usually be PL (purchases ledger), as the majority of payments will be to suppliers. The folio for DDs and SOs will usually be NL (nominal ledger), as these will not generally be payments to suppliers. The folio is usually inserted when the entry is being posted to the ledger and may also contain a number that references that particular account in the purchase ledger. Posting to ledgers will be explained later.

| Total: | The amount of the cheque, DD or SO will be entered here. |
| Creditor: | If the payment is to a supplier (creditor) then the amount is entered under the Creditors column. |

When you have completed this task, the Cash (Bank) Payments Book should look like the following:

COMPANY NAME: J.P. MURPHY ELECTRIC

Cash (Bank) Payments Book   Month: January ##

Date	Details	Cheque No	F	Total	Analysis				
					Creditors	Salaries	Rent	Petty Cash	Other
23/01/##	Philem Ireland	200101		2376.00	2376.00				

TASK M-11

Enter the details from the remittance advice on Source Documents, page 16 into the Cash (Bank) Payments Book.

TASK M-12

A direct debit of €325.00 was made for Rent on 30/01/##. Enter this payment into the Cash (Bank) Payments Book.

The entry of this payment is exactly the same as a payment to a supplier, except that the analysis is entered in the Rent column and not the Creditors column.

Note:

The entries in the Cash (Bank) Payments Book must be subsequently posted to the correct ledger account. The posting of these entries will be explained later.

Completed Cash (Bank) Payments Book for January after entering transactions

COMPANY NAME: J.P. MURPHY ELECTRIC									
Cash (Bank) Payments Book							Month: January ##		
Date	Details	Cheque No	F	Total	Analysis				
					Creditors	Salaries	Rent	Petty Cash	Other
23/01/##	Philem Ireland	200101		2376.00	2376.00				
27/01/##	Solon International	200102		6177.60	6177.60				
30/01/##	Rent Payment	DD		325.00			325.00		

Note:

The folio (F) reference (PL and NL in this case) is not usually entered until the figures are transferred to the ledger.

Summary Note

Remittance Advices and other Bank Payments are entered in the Cash (Bank)
Payments Book

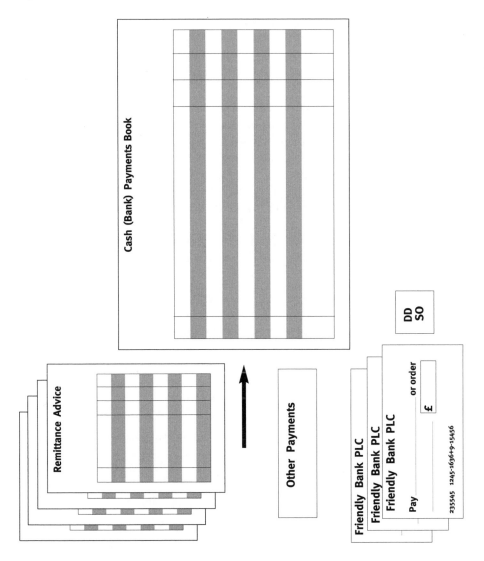

Petty Cash Book

Every business requires the purchase of small items, usually on a daily basis. It is not practical to issue an order for such items, receive an invoice and process the payment of them in the same way as is done for large items. It is also not practical to write a cheque for such small amounts.

Businesses normally retain a small amount of cash for the purchase of small items. The amount of this cash, at the start of each period, is referred to as 'petty cash imprest', and the petty cash book is used to record all items purchased using this cash.

All monies paid out of petty cash must be recorded on petty cash vouchers or dockets, which are used as the source documents for writing up the petty cash book. The VAT on such items is often not recorded, but if a business wishes to reclaim the VAT, then they must obtain a receipt for the payment, and record the VAT when entering the payment.

The source document is the petty cash voucher where payment was recorded. Each petty cash voucher is recorded on a separate row of the petty cash book.

We will now proceed with the task of writing up the petty cash book. You will require a Petty Cash Book (Source Documents page 189) in order to perform this task.

TASK M-13

Enter the petty cash voucher on Source Documents, page 17 into the Petty Cash Book.

This task requires you to enter the details from the petty cash voucher into the Petty Cash Book.

The petty cash book uses the following columns:

Date:	Enter the date of the purchase, which should be the date on the voucher.
Expenditure:	Enter the details of the item(s) purchased in this column.
Voucher:	Enter the voucher number for the expenditure.
Total:	Enter the total amount of the expenditure (including VAT where this is recorded).
VAT:	Enter the VAT amount if applicable.
Analysis:	Enter the breakdown of the items purchased into a number of different categories, e.g. – Post – Stationery – Cleaning – Miscellaneous expenses (anything that does not fit into any of the other analysis columns).

When you have completed this task, the petty cash book should look like the following:

	COMPANY NAME: J.P. MURPHY ELECTRIC							
Petty Cash Book							Month: January ##	

Date	Expenditure	Voucher Number	Total	VAT	Analysis			
					Post	Stationery	Cleaning	Misc. Exp.
05/01/##	Envelopes	1	4.00			4.00		

TASK M-14

Enter the petty cash vouchers on Source Documents pages 17–19 into the Petty Cash Book.

Note:

The entries in the Petty Cash Book must be subsequently posted to the correct ledger account. The posting of these entries will be explained later.

Completed Petty Cash Book for January after entering transactions

	COMPANY NAME: J.P. MURPHY ELECTRIC							
Petty Cash Book							Month: January ##	

Date	Expenditure	Voucher Number	Total	VAT	Analysis			
					Post	Stationery	Cleaning	Misc. Exp.
05/01/##	Envelopes	1	4.00			4.00		
09/01/##	Replace Window Glass	2	16.88	1.88				15.00
11/01/##	Postage Stamps	3	12.00		12.00			
13/01/##	Window Cleaning	4	5.00				5.00	
17/01/##	Box of Pens	5	9.50			9.50		

Summary Note

Petty Cash Vouchers are entered in the Petty Cash Book

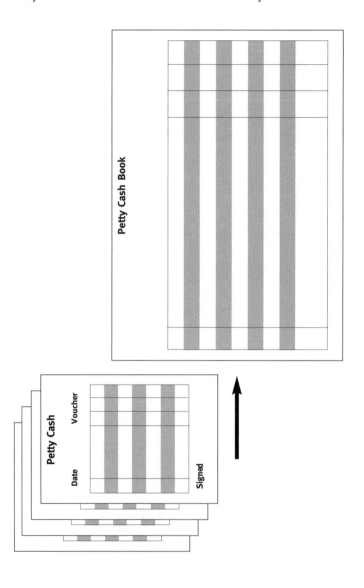

General Journal

The general journal is the sixth and final daybook. It is used to record any receipts or payments that do not readily fit into any of the other daybooks, e.g. capital investment, sale of an asset on credit. Very often there are no source documents used when making entries in the general journal. Entries in the general journal will occupy at least two rows. There will be at least one entry in the Debit column and at least one entry in the Credit column, with the total of both columns being equal. The number of entries in each column does not matter as long as the totals are equal. This is the essence of double entry that will be explained later. We will use the general journal to record the capital investment in a company.

The general journal is also used to record any internal bookkeeping that may need to be performed from time to time, e.g. accruals, prepayments, etc. We will not be dealing with these in this book.

We will now proceed with the next task. In order to perform this task you should have a General Journal (Source Documents, page 190).

TASK M-15

J.P. Murphy commenced business on 01/01/## with a capital investment of €15,000.00. €14,900.00 of this was deposited in their current bank account and €100.00 was placed in petty cash. Use the General Journal to record these entries.

There are no source documents used in the recording of these entries. The information is contained in the task and will require three rows in the general journal. The general journal uses the following columns:

Date:	Enter the date of the transaction.
Details:	Enter the details of this transaction. The details should be sufficient to identify the Nominal Ledger account to be posted to.
F:	The folio will be Nominal Ledger (NL) as the entries in the general journal will be posted directly into the Nominal Ledger. The folio is usually inserted when the entry is being posted to the ledger, and may also contain a number that references that particular account in the nominal ledger.
Debit:	Enter the debit amount for this entry if appropriate.
Credit:	Enter the credit amount for this entry if appropriate.

It is normal practice to add an explanation on the next line of the general journal explaining the entry in the journal.

When you have completed this task the General Journal should look like the following:

COMPANY NAME: J.P. MURPHY ELECTRIC				
General Journal				Month: January ##
Date	Details	F	Debit	Credit
01/01/##	Bank Current A/C		14,900.00	
01/01/##	Petty Cash		100.00	
01/01/##	Capital			15,000.00
	(Capital investment lodged)			

The entry of this capital investment requires the use of three rows in the general journal.

(i) The first entry is the record of the money lodged to the current account. This entry will be posted to the Bank Current Account in the Nominal Ledger. Since the Bank Account is a Debit account (which will be explained later), any monies lodged to the bank are recorded on the debit side of the journal.

(ii) The second entry is the record of the money retained in petty cash. This entry will be posted to the Petty Cash Account in the Nominal Ledger. Since the Petty Cash Account is a bank account, then this entry will be on the debit side of the journal.

(iii) The third entry in the record of the capital that was invested in the company. This entry will be posted to the Capital Account in the Nominal (General) Ledger. Since the Capital account is a credit account (which will be explained later) then this entry is entered in the Credit side of the journal.

The posting is usually completed by entering an explanation on the next line of the general journal.

Month End Calculations

The first task to be performed at the end of each month is to calculate the amount that was spent from petty cash and to restore the imprest to the correct amount. The company decides how much money should be in petty cash at the start of each month. This amount is called the 'imprest' and it must be restored at the end of each month before the month end calculations are performed. The petty cash imprest is restored from the bank current account, usually by cashing a cheque for the amount that was spent the previous week or month.

This cheque is recorded in the Cash (Bank) Payments Book in the same way as any other payment and is detailed as 'Restore Petty Cash Imprest'. The payment is analysed under the Petty Cash column. This will usually be the last entry in the Cash (Bank) Payments Book each month.

TASK M-16

On the 31/01/## cheque number 200103 was cashed to restore the petty cash imprest. Calculate the amount of this cheque and enter it into the Cash (Bank) Payments Book.

Completed Cash (Bank) Payments Book for January

COMPANY NAME: J.P. MURPHY ELECTRIC

Cash (Bank) Payments Book   Month: January ##

Date	Details	Cheque No	F	Total	Analysis				
					Creditors	Salaries	Rent	Petty Cash	Other
23/01/##	Philem Ireland	200101	PL	2376.00	2376.00				
27/01/##	Solon International	200102	PL	6177.60	6177.60				
30/01/##	Rent Payment	DD	NL	325.00			325.00		
31/01/##	Restore Petty Cash Imprest	200103	NL	47.38				47.38	

At the end of each month, the columns in the daybooks that contain money amounts are totalled and cross-checked to ensure accuracy and for posting to the ledgers.

TASK M-17
Total all the daybooks and cross-check the figures.

Cross checking of the daybooks should be performed as follows:

Sales/Sales Returns Daybook
   This book is cross-checked as follows:

	Total Net Amount @ 21%
+	Total Net Amount @ 12.5%
+	Total VAT Amount
=	Total of Total column

A second cross-check is:

	Total VAT Amount
+	Total Sales
+	Total Repairs
=	Total of Total column

Purchases/Purchases Returns Daybook
   This book is cross-checked as follows:

	Total Goods for Resale
+	Total Goods Not for Resale
+	Total VAT Amount
=	Total of Total column

A second cross-check is

	Total VAT Amount
+	Total Purchases
+	Total Electricity
+	Total Telephone
+	Total Fixtures & Fittings
=	Total of Total column

Cash Receipts (Bank Lodgement) Book
   This book is cross-checked as follows:

	Total Cash Sales
+	Total Debtors
+	Total Other
=	Total of Total column

Cash (Bank) Payments Book

This book is cross-checked as follows:

	Total Creditors
+	Total Salaries
+	Total Rent
+	Total Petty Cash
+	Total Other
=	Total of Total column

Petty Cash Book

This book is cross-checked as follows:

	Total Post
+	Total Stationery
+	Total Cleaning
+	Total Miscellaneous Expenses
+	Total VAT
=	Total of Total column

General Journal

In this book the total of the Debit column should equal the total of the Credit column.

Completed Daybooks

Sales/Sales Returns Daybook   Month: January ##__

Date	Customer	F	Inv./Cr. Nt. Number	Total	Net Amount @ 20%	@ 12.5%	VAT Amount	Analysis Sales	Repairs
06/01/##	James Mahon		1001	453.60	378.00		75.60	378.00	
07/01/##	The Electrical Shop		1002	1847.70	1512.00	29.60	306.10	1512.00	29.60
09/01/##	New Age Contractors		1003	4952.85	4058.00	74.00	820.85	4058.00	74.00
11/01/##	Cash Sale		1004	49.95		44.40	5.55		44.40
12/01/##	Tomorrow's Electronics		1005	4279.50	3483.00	88.80	707.70	3483.00	88.80
13/01/##	New Age Contractors		1006	(549.60)	(458.00)		(91.60)	(458.00)	
			Totals	1103.00	8973.00	236.80	1824.20	8973.00	236.80

Cash Receipts (Bank Lodgement) Book   Month: January ##

Date	Details	Lodge No.	F	Bank	Cash Sales	Debtors	Other
11/01/##	Cash Sale	101		49.95	49.95		
12/01/##	James Mahon (chq 204587)	102		453.60		453.60	
21/01/##	The Electrical Shop (chq 215687)	103		1847.70		1847.70	
22/01/##	New Age Contractors (chq 272357)	104		4403.25		4403.25	
25/01/##	Tomorrow's Electronics (chq 467832)	105		4000.00		4000.00	
		Totals		10754.50	49.95	10704.55	

Purchases/Purchases Returns Daybook   Month: January ##

Date	Supplier	F	Inv./Cr.Nt. Number	Total	Goods for Resale Net@20%	Net@12.5%	Goods N for R Net@20%	VAT Amnt	Analysis Purchases	Elec.	Tel.	Fix. & Fit.
02/01/##	Solon Intl		216457	6336.00	5280.00			1056.00	5280.00			
03/01/##	Philem Irl		78542	2376.00	1980.00			396.00	1980.00			
12/01/##	Mod. Com.			66.90			55.75	11.15			55.75	
13/01/##	Solon Int		5347	(158.40)	(132.00)			(26.40)	(132.00)			
			Totals	8620.50	7128.00		55.75	1436.75	7128.00		55.75	

Cash (Bank) Payments Book   Month: January

Date	Details	Cheque No	F	Total	Creditors	Salaries	Rent	Petty Cash	Other
23/01/##	Philem Ireland	200101		2376.00	2376.00				
27/01/##	Solon International	200102		6177.60	6177.60				
30/01/##	Rent Payment	DD		325.00			325.00		
31/01/##	Restore Petty Cash	200103		47.38				47.38	
		Totals		8925.98	8553.60		325.00	47.38	

Petty Cash Book   Month: January

Date	Expenditure	Voucher Number	Total	VAT	Post	Stationery	Cleaning	Misc. Exp.
05/01/##	Envelopes	1	4.00			4.00		
09/01/##	Replace Window Glass	2	16.88	1.88				15.00
11/01/##	Postage Stamps	3	12.00		12.00			
13/01/##	Window Cleaning	4	5.00				5.00	
17/01/##	Box of Pens	5	9.50			9.50		
		Totals	47.38	1.88	12.00	13.50	5.00	15.00

General Journal   Month: January

Date	Details	F	Debit	Credit
01/01/##	Bank Current A/C		14,900.00	
01/01/##	Petty Cash		100.00	
01/01/##	Capital			15,000.00
	(Capital investment lodged)			

3 Ledgers

Ledgers are used to assemble all the details about one customer, supplier, income, expense, asset, liability and owner's equity in one place. The information from the daybooks will be posted to an individual account in the appropriate ledger. Each daybook is used for a single month and then a new daybook is started for the next month. In the case of ledgers, each customer, supplier, etc., requires a separate sheet (ledger), and the same sheet is used until it is full and then another one is added. The information for each ledger account is therefore continuous.

When writing up the ledgers, we will be using the continuous balance method. The continuous balance method calculates the balance in an account each time an entry is made in that account. With this method there is no further calculation required in order to determine an account balance.

There are three ledgers used for posting the various daybooks to, namely:

Sales (Debtors') Ledger	–	Customer accounts
Purchases (Creditors') Ledger	–	Supplier accounts
Nominal (General) Ledger	–	Company accounts, i.e. income, expenses, assets, liabilities and owner's equity

Using the continuous balance method, all ledgers have three columns for entering money amounts: Debit (Dr), Credit (Cr) and Balance (Bal). It is essential that the amount be entered into the correct column and the correct method be used to calculate the balance as will be explained when dealing with each individual ledger.

Posting from the daybooks uses the double entry system. This means that every entry in the daybooks must be posted to two separate accounts in the ledgers. It must be posted once on the Debit side of an account and once on the Credit side of another account. In most cases the second posting will not be as an individual amount, but rather as a total from a daybook, but it is still being posted the second time.

An example of this double entry is when a sale is recorded to a customer. The sale is initially recorded in the sales daybook. This entry is subsequently posted on the Debit side of the customer's account in the Sales Ledger. The double entry in this case is that the goods sold to this customer are posted as part of the Total Sales on the Credit side of the Sales account in the Nominal Ledger, and the VAT on this sale is posted as part of the Total VAT on the Credit side of the VAT account in the Nominal Ledger. Therefore the sale is posted twice, once as a Debit and once as a Credit. All entries in the daybooks will be posted twice and you should be able to trace the double entry of all entries in the daybooks.

Sales (Debtors') Ledger

The record of all invoices and credit notes issued to a customer are recorded in the Sales/Sales Returns Daybook. All of the receipts from customers are recorded in the Cash Receipts (Bank Lodgement) book. However, neither of these books indicate how much any individual customer owes or how much they bought over a period of time.

The Sales (Debtors') Ledger is used to keep a record of all credit customers (Debtors). Some businesses will also have an account named 'Cash Sale', which is used to record all cash sales. This account is treated as if it were a single customer, with entries recorded in the same way as they would be for any individual customer. All the entries in the sales daybook and the receipts from customers recorded in the Cash Receipts Book are posted to the Sales Ledger. Each customer has a separate page (sheet) in the Sales Ledger where all the sales and receipts for that particular customer are recorded. (All cash sales will be entered into a single account called 'Cash Sales'). This, then, is the next level of recording sales in the company.

We will now continue our work by posting the entries in the Sales/Sales Returns Daybook to the Sales Ledger.

TASK M-18

Post the first entry in the Sales/Sales Returns Daybook to the Sales Ledger.

You will require a sales ledger card (Source Documents page 191) for this task.

The source document for this task is the Sales/Sales Returns Daybook. Entries in the daybook should be posted to the Sales Ledger in date order. It is normal to post the entries in the cash receipts book at the same time so that the dates will be in order for each customer, but we will leave this until later.

The Sales Ledger has a number of columns as follows:

Date:	This is the date of the Invoice, Credit Note or receipt as entered in the daybook.
Details:	The details of the entry in the ledger, e.g.
	Sales Entry from the sales daybook. This entry may also contain the invoice number.
	Returns Entry from the sales returns daybook. This entry may also contain the credit note number.
	Receipt Entry of receipt from the cash receipts book. This entry may also contain the cheque number.
F:	This stands for folio and is the reference for this posting in the ledger. The folio indicates where this posting originated, e.g.
	SB Sales/Sales Returns Book
	CRB Cash Receipts (Bank Lodgement) Book

The folio is usually inserted when the entry is being posted to the ledger and may also contain a number that references that particular account in the Sales Ledger. Posting to ledgers will be explained later.

Dr:	This stands for Debit and is the Debit amount of this posting. This is nearly always a sale. The amount is the total amount from the Total column.
	Note: Debit Sales in a Sales Ledger account
Cr:	This stands for Credit and is the Credit amount of this posting. This is usually either returns or a receipt of money. The amount is the total amount from the Total column.
	Note: Credit Receipts and Returns in a Sales Ledger account
Bal:	This stands for balance and is the running balance for this account. The balance is usually positive and is the amount that this customer owes us. It is calculated each time an entry is made in the ledger as follows:
	Bal = Previous Bal + Dr - Cr

Note:

In the Sales Ledger:
Debits (Dr) are Positive +
Credits (Cr) are Negative −

When you have completed this task, James Mahon's Sales Ledger should look like the following:

	COMPANY NAME: J.P. MURPHY ELECTRIC				
Sales (Debtors') Ledger			Debtor (Customer): James Mahon		

Date	Details	F	Dr	Cr	Bal
06/01/##	Sales (Invoice 100001)	SB	453.60		453.60

TASK M-19

Post the remaining entries in the Sales/Sales Returns Daybook to the Sales Ledger.

You will require a number of sales ledger cards (Source Documents page 191) for this task.

When a credit note is being posted the amount is posted in the Cr column. The amount is not placed in brackets, as the Cr column is a minus column in the sales ledger. The detail for a credit note would normally be "Returns (credit note no. #####)".

When all the individual entries in the Sales/Sales Returns Daybook have been posted, it is normal practice to post the totals to the nominal ledger, thereby completing the double entry. However, since we have not dealt with the nominal ledger yet, we will leave that task until later.

TASK M-20

Post the first entry in the Cash Receipts (Bank Lodgement) Book to the Sales Ledger.

The source document for this task is the Cash Receipts (Bank Lodgement) Book. The posting of the receipts from the cash receipts book is exactly the same as posting the Sales and Returns. Post the individual entries in the cash receipts book to the Credit column of the customers account in the Sales Ledger. Receipt amounts are posted in the credit column because they must be subtracted from the amount this customer owes the company.

Again it is normal practice to post the totals to the nominal ledger, thereby completing the double entry, but we will leave this until we are dealing with the Nominal Ledger.

When you have completed this task, James Mahon's Sales Ledger should look like the following:

	COMPANY NAME: J.P. MURPHY ELECTRIC				
Sales (Debtors') Ledger				Debtor (Customer): James Mahon	

Date	Details	F	Dr	Cr	Bal
06/01/##	Sales (Invoice 100001)	SB	453.60		453.60
10/01/##	Receipt (cheque 204587)	CRB		453.60	0.00

TASK M-21

Post the remaining entries in the Cash Receipts (Bank Lodgement) Book to the Sales Ledger.

Completed Sales Ledgers

When you have completed this task, the remaining Sales Ledgers should look like the following:

	COMPANY NAME: J.P. MURPHY ELECTRIC				
Sales (Debtors') Ledger				Debtor (Customer): The Electrical Shop	

Date	Details	F	Dr	Cr	Bal
07/01/##	Sales (Invoice 100002)	SB	1847.70		1847.70
21/01/##	Receipt (cheque no 215687)	CRB		1847.70	0.00

	COMPANY NAME: J.P. MURPHY ELECTRIC				
Sales (Debtors') Ledger				Debtor (Customer): New Age Contractors	

Date	Details	F	Dr	Cr	Bal
09/01/##	Sales (Invoice 100003)	SB	4952.85		4952.85
13/01/##	Returns (credit note 100006)	SB		549.60	4403.25
22/01/##	Receipt (cheque no 272357)	CRB		4403.25	0.00

COMPANY NAME: J.P. MURPHY ELECTRIC					
Sales (Debtors') Ledger			Debtor (Customer): Tomorrow's Electronics		

Date	Details	F	Dr	Cr	Bal
12/01/##	Sales (Invoice 100005)	SB	4279.50		4279.50
25/01/##	Receipt (cheque no 467832)	CRB		4000.00	279.50

Summary Note

Sales Summary from Source Documents to Sales Ledger

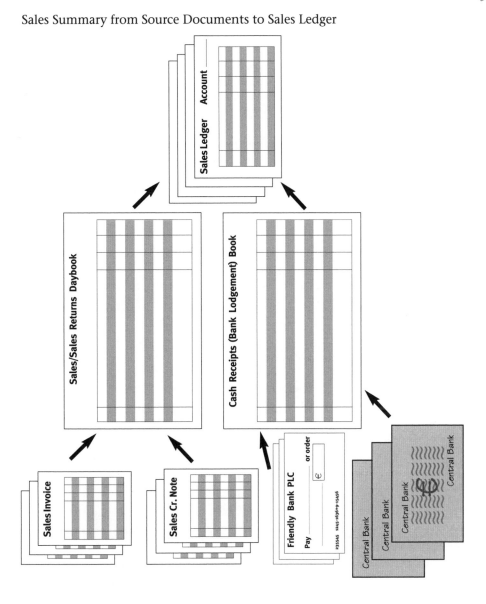

Purchases (Creditors') Ledger

The record of all invoices and credit notes received from suppliers are recorded in the Purchases/Purchases Returns Daybook. All the payments made by the company are recorded in the Cash (Bank) Payments book. However neither of these books indicate how much the company owes any particular supplier or how much the company purchased from a supplier over a period of time.

The Purchases (Creditors') Ledger is used to keep a record of all suppliers (creditors). All the individual entries in the Purchases Daybook and the payments made to suppliers, recorded in the Cash (Bank) Payments book, are posted to the Purchases Ledger and the totals are posted to the Nominal Ledger. Each supplier has a separate page (sheet) in the Purchases Ledger where all the purchases and payments for that particular supplier are recorded. This, then, is the next level of recording purchases in the company.

We will now continue our work by posting the entries in the Purchases/Purchases Returns Daybook to the Purchases Ledger.

TASK M-22

Post the first entry in the Purchases/Purchases Returns Daybook to the Purchases Ledger.

You will require a purchases ledger card (page 192) for this task.

The source document for this task is the Purchases/Purchases Returns Daybook. Entries in the daybook should be posted to the purchases ledger in date order. It is normal to post the entries from the 'Creditors' column in the Cash Payments book at the same time so that the dates will be in order for each supplier, but we will leave this until later.

The Purchases Ledger has a number of columns as follows:

Date:	This is the date of the invoice, credit note or payment as entered in the daybook.
Details:	The details of the entry in the ledger, e.g.
	Purchases Entry from the Purchases daybook. This entry may also include an invoice number.
	Returns Entry from the Purchases Returns daybook. This entry may also include a credit note number.
	Payment Entry of payment from the Cash Payments book. This entry may also include the cheque number.
F:	This stands for folio and is the reference for this posting in the ledger. The folio indicates where this posting originated, e.g.
	PB Purchases/purchases returns Book
	CPB Cash (Bank) Payments Book

The folio is usually inserted when the entry is being posted to the ledger and may also contain a number that references that particular account in the sales ledger. Posting to ledgers will be explained later.

Note:

In the Purchases Ledger:
Debits (Dr) are Negative -
Credits (Cr) are Positive +

When you have completed this task, Solon International's Purchases Ledger account should look like the following:

COMPANY NAME: J.P. MURPHY ELECTRIC						
Purchases (Creditors') Ledger				Creditor (Supplier): Solon International		
Date	Details	F	Dr	Cr	Bal	
02/01/##	Purchases (Invoice 216457)	PB		6388.80	6388.80	

TASK M-23

Post the remaining entries in the Purchases/Purchases Returns Daybook to the Purchases Ledger.

When a credit note is being posted the amount is posted in the Dr column. The amount is not placed in brackets, as the Dr column is a minus column in the purchases ledger. The detail for a credit note would normally be Returns (credit note no. #####).

TASK M-24

Post the first entry in the Cash (Bank) Payments Book to the Purchases Ledger.

The source document for this task is the Cash (Bank) Payments Book. The posting of the payments from the cash payments book is exactly the same as posting the Purchases and Returns. Payment amounts are posted in the debit column because the must be subtracted from the amount the company owes this supplier.

When you have completed this task, Solon International's Purchases Ledger account should look like the following:

COMPANY NAME: J.P. MURPHY ELECTRIC					
Purchases (Creditors') Ledger			Creditor (Supplier): Solon International		
Date	**Details**	**F**	**Dr**	**Cr**	**Bal**
02/01/##	Purchases (Invoice 216457)	PB		6336.00	6336.00
13/01/##	Returns (Credit Note No: 5347)	PB	158.40		6177.60
27/01/##	Payment (cheque no: 200102)	CPB	6170.60		0.00

TASK M-25

Post the remaining entries in the Cash (Bank) Payments Book to the Purchases Ledger.

Completed Purchases Ledgers

When you have completed this task, the remaining Purchase Ledgers should look like the following:

COMPANY NAME: J.P. MURPHY ELECTRIC					
Purchases (Creditors') Ledger			Creditor (Supplier): Philem Ireland		
Date	**Details**	**F**	**Dr**	**Cr**	**Bal**
03/01/##	Purchases (Invoice 78542)	PB		2376.00	2376.60
23/01/##	Payment (cheque no 200101)	CPB	2376.60		0.00

COMPANY NAME: J.P. MURPHY ELECTRIC					
Purchases (Creditors') Ledger			Creditor (Supplier): Modern Communications		
Date	**Details**	**F**	**Dr**	**Cr**	**Bal**
12/01/##	Purchases	PB		66.90	66.90

Summary Note

Purchases Summary from Source Documents to Purchases Ledger

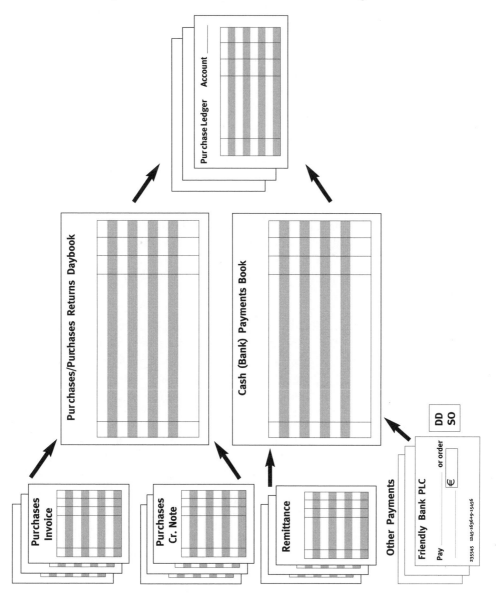

Nominal (General) Ledgers

The Nominal (General) Ledger consists of a number of accounts that are used to record the income, expenditure, assets, liabilities and owner's equity in the company. Every transaction that occurs in the company must eventually be recorded in a nominal ledger. Figures are transferred from the daybooks and Sales and Purchases Ledgers. The figures are normally posted on a monthly basis and are usually totals for the month, as the individual figures will have already been entered in the Sales and Purchases Ledgers. The balance figures in the nominal accounts are used in producing a trial balance, which we will be doing later.

Nominal accounts will be one of five possible types: income, expense, asset, liability or owner equity, as shown in the table below. Each type of account will be either a Debit (Dr) or Credit (Cr) account. This means that if an account is a Credit account, then the balance in that account will normally be a Credit amount. If an account is a Debit account, then the balance in that account will normally be a Debit amount. However, a negative balance will result in a Debit account having a Credit balance instead of a Debit balance, and vice versa.

Examples of Nominal Accounts include the following:

TYPE	DR OR CR	EXAMPLES
Income	Cr	When goods or services are sold by a company, the monies received are referred to as 'income' and are recorded in an Income account. Examples of income accounts are: sales, repairs, income, rent received and investment income.
Expense	Dr	Any monies paid out by a business for the purchase of goods, materials or services required for the day to day running of the business are referred to as expenses and are recorded in an Expense account. Expense accounts may be divided into two categories: Cost of Sales This is a particular type of account that contains all monies paid out which relate directly to the cost of selling goods. Examples of these accounts are: purchases, packaging and delivery costs. Expense Any other monies paid out for services on a regular basis. Examples of these accounts are: electricity, telephone, rent paid, salaries paid, post, stationery, cleaning and miscellaneous expenses.

Asset	Dr	All items or monies that are owned by the business are regarded as assets and are recorded in Asset accounts. Asset accounts may be divided into two categories Current Assets These are assets that relate to items that change on a regular basis, normally daily. Examples of asset accounts are: debtors, bank, petty cash and stock. Fixed Assets These are assets that the company owns, but which do not change regularly. Examples of fixed asset accounts are: machinery, fixtures & fittings and vehicles.
Liability	Cr	Any monies owed by a business at any time are referred to as liabilities and are recorded in a Liability account. Examples of liability accounts are: creditors, VAT payable, PRSI payable and bank overdraft.
Owner Equity	Cr	All monies invested in a business, and profits retained by the business, are recorded in an Owner Equity account. Examples of owner equity accounts are: capital, shares and retained profit.

Calculating the Balance in an Account

Every time an entry is made in an account then the Balance must be calculated in a similar manner to the sales and purchases ledger. However in the case of the nominal ledger some accounts are credit accounts and some accounts are debit accounts. This means that before you calculate the balance you must firstly ascertain if the account is a debit or credit account. The various account types are shown in the above table.

In the case of Debit accounts, Debits are positive (+) and Credits are Negative (-).

In the case of Credit accounts, Credits are positive (+) and Debits are Negative (-).

Writing Up the Nominal (General) Ledger

The writing up of the Nominal Ledger is very similar to the Sales and Purchase Ledger, and we will be using the continuous balance method.

The Nominal Ledger has a number of columns into which entries should be made as follows:

Date:	The date of the entry in the ledger. This is usually the last day of the month.
Details:	The details of the entry in the ledger.
F:	This stands for folio and is the reference for this posting in the ledger, i.e. where this posting came from.
Dr:	If the account is a Debit account then the posting will normally have an entry in the Debit column.
Cr:	If the account is a Credit account then the posting will normally have an entry in the Credit column.
Bal:	This is the running balance for the account. The balance is usually positive and will be a Debit or Credit amount depending on the type of account. However, a negative balance will be indicated by placing the figure in brackets as in the daybooks, and usually by writing the letters Dr or Cr in the right margin to indicate that the balance is opposite what is usual for that type of account.

We will now proceed with the task of writing up the Nominal (General) Ledger Accounts. You will need a number of nominal ledger cards (Source Documents, page 193) for this task.

TASK M-26

Post the totals from the General Journal into the Nominal (General) Ledger.

This is the easiest daybook to transfer figures from because the figures are already written in the correct columns. When posting from the General Journal into the Nominal Ledger, debits are posted as Debits and credits are posted as Credits.

The first entry in the General Journal is Capital. This means that we need a Capital account.

When this entry is made, the Nominal (General) Ledger Capital Account should look like the following:

COMPANY NAME: J.P. MURPHY ELECTRIC

Nominal (General) Ledger   Nominal Account: Capital

Date	Details	F	Dr	Cr	Bal
31/01/##	Initial Capital Investment	GJ		15,000.00	15,000.00

The second entry is the Bank Current A/C so we need a Bank Current A/C account Nominal Ledger.

When this entry is made the Nominal (General) Ledger Bank Current A/C account should look like the following:

COMPANY NAME: J.P. MURPHY ELECTRIC						
Nominal (General) Ledger				Nominal Account: Bank Current A/C		
Date	Details	F	Dr	Cr	Bal
31/01/##	Capital Investment Lodged	GJ	14,900.00		14,900.00

The third entry is to Petty Cash. This is entered in the Petty Cash Account in the same way as the above.

When this entry is made the Nominal (General) Ledger Petty Cash account should look like the following:

COMPANY NAME: J.P. MURPHY ELECTRIC						
Nominal (General) Ledger				Nominal Account: Petty Cash		
Date	Details	F	Dr	Cr	Bal
31/01/##	Capital Kept for Petty Cash	GJ	100.00		100.00

We will now continue with the task of posting the Sales/Sales Returns Daybook to the Nominal (General) Ledger.

TASK M-27

Post the totals from the Sales/Sales Returns Daybook into the Nominal (General) Ledger.

The following totals must be posted to the Debit or Credit columns of the individual nominal accounts

VAT Total   The VAT Payable account is a Credit account because it is a liability account and will normally have a credit balance. However, it is one of the accounts that will have entries in

both the Debit and Credit columns. The VAT total from the Sales/Sales Returns Daybook is posted in the Credit column as this is the VAT which is collected and is due to be paid to the collector general.
Note: VAT collected is Credit.

Sales Total   The Sales account is a Credit account, so the Sales total is simply posted to the Cr column of the Sales account.

Repairs Total   The repairs account is a Credit account so the Repairs total is simply posted to the Cr column of the Repairs account.

When you have completed this task the Sales account in the Nominal (General) Ledger should look like the following:

COMPANY NAME: J.P. MURPHY ELECTRIC						
Nominal (General) Ledger					Nominal Account: Sales	
Date	Details	F	Dr	Cr	Bal	
31/01/##	Total Sales (January ##)	SDB		8973.00	8973.00	

The Repairs and VAT accounts will look similar to the Sales account.

Note:

The individual rows of the Sales/Sales Returns Daybook have already been posted to the individual debtors accounts in the Sales Ledger. This means that every entry in the sales/sales returns daybook has been posted to two ledger accounts, once on the Debit side and once on the Credit side.

The next task is to post the Purchases/Purchases Returns Daybook to the Nominal (General) Ledger.

TASK M-28

Post the totals from the Purchases/Purchases Returns Daybook to the Nominal (General) Ledger.

The following totals must be posted to the Debit or Credit columns of the individual nominal accounts

VAT Total   The VAT payable account is a Credit account as it is a liability account and will normally have a Credit balance. However when posting from the Purchases/Purchases Returns Daybook, the amount is posted in the **Debit** column as this is VAT which the company has paid out and which it is reclaiming from the collector general. This amount is subtracted from the previous balance amount in order to obtain the Balance figure.

Note: VAT paid out is Debit.

Purchases Total	The purchases account is a Debit account so the Purchases total is simply posted to the Dr column of the Purchases account.
Electricity Total	The Electricity account is a Debit account so the Electricity total is simply posted to the Dr column of the Electricity account. Since there was no entry in the Electricity column you may skip this account until next month.
Telephone Total	The Telephone account is a Debit account so the Telephone total is simply posted to the Dr column of the Telephone account.
Fixture & Fittings	The Fixtures & Fittings account is a Debit Account so the Fixtures & Fittings total is simply posted to the Dr column of the Fixtures & Fittings account. Since there was no entry in the Fixtures & Fittings column, you may skip this account until next month.

When you have completed this task, the VAT account in the Nominal (General) Ledger should now look like the following:

COMPANY NAME: J.P. MURPHY ELECTRIC

Nominal (General) Ledger   Nominal Account: VAT Payable

Date	Details	F	Dr	Cr	Bal
31/01/##	VAT on Sales (Jan ##)	SDB		1824.20	1824.20
31/01/##	VAT on Purchases (Jan ##)	PDB	1436.75		387.45

The Purchases Account should look like the following:

		COMPANY NAME: J.P. MURPHY ELECTRIC				
Nominal (General) Ledger				Nominal Account: Purchases		

Date	Details	F	Dr	Cr	Bal
31/01/##	Total Purchases (January ##)	PDB	7128.00		7128.00

The Telephone account is another expense account and therefore the figure will be posted in the Debit column and will therefore the account should look similar to the Purchases account.

Note:

The individual rows of the Purchases/Purchases Returns Daybook have already been posted to the individual creditors accounts in the Purchase Ledger. This means that every entry in the Purchases/Purchases Returns Daybook has been posted to two ledger accounts, once on the Debit side and once on the Credit side.

The next task is to post the Cash Receipts (Bank Lodgement) Book to the Nominal (General) Ledger.

TASK M-29

Post the totals from the Cash Receipts (Bank Lodgement) Book to the Nominal (General) Ledger.

In this case the only figure that we need to post is the total of the Bank column to the Bank Current A/C in the nominal ledger. This account is another account where entries are made in the Debit and Credit columns. The Bank Current A/C is a Debit account and therefore the total from the Cash Receipts (Bank Lodgement) Book is posted to the Debit column as it is money received by the company.

Note:

Money lodged into a bank account is debit.

The next task is to post the Cash (Bank) Payments Book to the Nominal (General) Ledger.

TASK M-30

Post the totals from the Cash (Bank) Payments Book to the Nominal (General) Ledger.

The following totals must be posted to the Debit or Credit columns of the individual nominal accounts

Total Total	The Total of all payments must be posted to the Bank Current A/C in the Nominal Ledger. Even though Bank Current A/C is a Debit account, the total from the Cash (Bank) Payments Book is posted to the Credit column as it is money paid out by the company and therefore reduces the amount in the Bank.
Salaries Total	The Salaries account is a Debit account, so the Salaries total is simply posted to the Dr column of the Salaries account. Since there was no entry in the Salaries column you may skip this account until next month.
Rent Total	The Rent account is a Debit Account so the Rent total is simply posted to the Dr column of the Rent Account.
Petty Cash Total	This is the money that has been transferred to Petty Cash to restore the imprest. The Petty Cash account is a Debit account, so the Petty Cash total is simply posted to the Dr column of the Petty Cash account, as this is money paid into petty cash, in the same way as money paid **into** the bank account is posted to the Debit side.
Other	Entries in this column should have a note written in the side margin indicating what the payment was for, and the entry would then be posted to the relevant account. Since there was no entry in the Other column, you may skip this account.

When you have completed this task the Bank Current A/C in the Nominal (General) Ledger should look like the following:

COMPANY NAME: J.P. MURPHY ELECTRIC					
Nominal (General) Ledger			Nominal Account: Bank Current A/C		

Date	Details	F	Dr	Cr	Bal
31/01/##	Capital Investment	GJ	14,900.00		14,900.00
31/01/##	Total Lodgements (Jan ##)	CRB	10,754.50		25654.45
31/01/##	Total Payments (Jan ##)	CPB		8,925.98	16,728.52

The final daybook to be posted to the Nominal (General) Ledger is the Petty Cash Book.

TASK M-31
Post the totals from the Petty Cash Book to the Nominal (General) Ledger.

The following totals must be posted to the Debit or Credit columns of the individual nominal accounts:

Total Total	The Total amount of petty cash payments for the period is posted to the Credit side of the Petty Cash account. The Petty Cash account is a Debit account, but in the same way as payments out of the bank account are posted to the Credit side, so the payments out of petty cash are posted to the Cr column of the Petty Cash account.
VAT Total	The VAT payable account is a Credit account, as it is a liability account and will normally have a Credit balance. However, when posting from the Petty Cash book, the amount is posted in the **Debit** column, in the same way as VAT on purchase is entered, as this is VAT which the company has paid out and which it is reclaiming from the Collector General. This amount is subtracted from the previous balance amount in order to obtain the Balance figure.
Post Total	The Post account is a Debit account, so the Post total is posted to the Dr column of the Post account.
Stationery Total	The Stationery account is a Debit account, so the Stationery total is posted to the Dr column of the Stationery account.
Cleaning Total	The Cleaning account is a Debit account, so the Cleaning total is posted to the Dr column of the Cleaning account.
Misc. Exp. Total	The Miscellaneous Expenses account is a Debit account, so the Misc. Exp. total is posted to the Dr column of the Miscellaneous Expenses Account.

Completed Nominal Ledgers

When you have completed this task, the Nominal Ledgers should look like the following:

COMPANY NAME: J.P. MURPHY ELECTRIC

Nominal (General) Ledger   Nominal Account: Sales

Date	Details	F	Dr	Cr	Bal
31/01/##	Sales (January ##)	SDB		8973.00	8973.00

COMPANY NAME: J.P. MURPHY ELECTRIC

Nominal (General) Ledger   Nominal Account: Repairs

Date	Details	F	Dr	Cr	Bal
31/01/##	Repairs (January ##)	SDB		236.80	236.80

COMPANY NAME: J.P. MURPHY ELECTRIC

Nominal (General) Ledger   Nominal Account: Purchases

Date	Details	F	Dr	Cr	Bal
31/01/##	Purchases (January ##)	PDB	7128.00		7128.00

COMPANY NAME: J.P. MURPHY ELECTRIC

Nominal (General) Ledger   Nominal Account: Telephone

Date	Details	F	Dr	Cr	Bal
31/01/##	Telephone (January ##)	PDB	55.75		55.75

COMPANY NAME: J.P. MURPHY ELECTRIC

Nominal (General) Ledger   Nominal Account: Rent

Date	Details	F	Dr	Cr	Bal
31/01/##	Rent (January ##)	CPB	325.00		325.00

COMPANY NAME: J.P. MURPHY ELECTRIC

Nominal (General) Ledger   Nominal Account: Post

Date	Details	F	Dr	Cr	Bal
31/01/##	Post (January ##)	PCB	12.00		12.00

COMPANY NAME: J.P. MURPHY ELECTRIC

Nominal (General) Ledger   Nominal Account: Stationery

Date	Details	F	Dr	Cr	Bal
31/01/##	Stationery (January ##)	PCB	13.50		13.50

COMPANY NAME: J.P. MURPHY ELECTRIC

Nominal (General) Ledger

Nominal Account: Cleaning

Date	Details	F	Dr	Cr	Bal
31/01/##	Cleaning (January ##)	PCB	5.00		5.00

COMPANY NAME: J.P. MURPHY ELECTRIC

Nominal (General) Ledger

Nominal Account: Miscellaneous Expenses

Date	Details	F	Dr	Cr	Bal
31/01/##	Misc. Exp. (January ##)	PCB	15.00		15.00

COMPANY NAME: J.P. MURPHY ELECTRIC

Nominal (General) Ledger

Nominal Account: Bank Current A/C

Date	Details	F	Dr	Cr	Bal
01/01/##	Capital Investment	GJ	14,900.00		14,900.00
31/01/##	Bank Lodgements (Jan ##)	CRB	10,754.50		25,654.50
31/01/##	Cash Payments (Jan ##)	CPB		8,925.98	16,728.52

COMPANY NAME: J.P. MURPHY ELECTRIC

Nominal (General) Ledger   Nominal Account: Petty Cash

Date	Details	F	Dr	Cr	Bal
01/01/##	Opening Balance	GJ	100.00		100.00
31/01/##	Total Payments (Jan ##)	PCB		47.38	52.62
31/01/##	Restore Imprest	BPB	47.38		100.00

COMPANY NAME: J.P. MURPHY ELECTRIC

Nominal (General) Ledger   Nominal Account: VAT Payable

Date	Details	F	Dr	Cr	Bal
31/01/##	VAT on Sales (Jan ##)	SDB		1,824.20	1,824.20
31/01/##	VAT on Purchases (Jan ##)	PDB	1,436.75		387.45
31/01/##	VAT on Petty Cash Purchases	PCB	1.88		385.57

COMPANY NAME: J.P. MURPHY ELECTRIC

Nominal (General) Ledger   Nominal Account: Capital

Date	Details	F	Dr	Cr	Bal
01/01/##	Capital Investment	GJ		15,000.00	15,000.00

Summary Note

Totals from daybooks are posted to the Nominal Ledgers

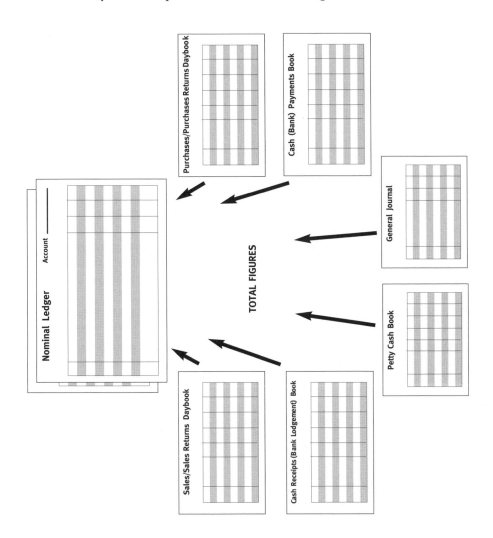

4 Trial Balance

At regular intervals, usually every month, a company will perform a trial balance. A trial balance is a list of all Nominal accounts with the balance in each account listed. The totals from the Sales and Purchase Ledger are also included where debtors and creditors control accounts are not used.

Since every transaction has been entered into two Ledger accounts, once on the debit side and once on the credit side, then the total of all the debits should equal the total of all the credits. A trial balance is used to check that this is correct. A trial balance does not ensure that all entries are correct; it simply checks that the total of the debits equals the total of the credits. However, this procedure does usually show up any errors that have been made over the period since the last trial balance.

If a trial balance does not balance, i.e. the total of the debits does not equal the total of the credits, then the error may be corrected or a balancing amount posted to a suspense account and the correction made later. In any event, the correction should be made before the next trial balance is performed.

TASK M-34

Complete a VAT 3 form for the month of January ##.

The term 'as at' means from the start of the financial year up to the stated date. In this case, since we have only completed the first month, this will mean that there will only be one month's figures in the trial balance.

Procedure for performing a trial balance

The figures for a trial balance are taken from the closing balances from all of the Nominal (General) Ledger accounts. The totals of the balances from the Sales Ledger accounts and Purchases Ledger accounts are also included in a trial balance. The Nominal accounts are assembled by type, i.e. Income, Expense, Asset, Liability and Owner's Equity. A list is then made of all the accounts together with a debit and credit column, as shown below. Entries for Debtors and Creditors is also made. If the account is a Debit account, then the balance figure is written in the Debit column, and if the account is a

Credit account, then the Balance figure is written in the Credit column. The
total of the debtors is a Debit amount, and the total of the creditors is a
Credit amount. Care should be taken that an account balance is not negative,
as in such a case the balance figure is written in the opposite column.

The complete trial balance is shown below.

J.P. MURPHY ELECTRIC

TRIAL BALANCE AS AT 31/01/##

	Debit	Credit
Sales		8,973.00
Repairs		236.80
Purchases	7,128.00	
Rent	325.00	
Telephone	55.75	
Post	12.00	
Stationery	13.50	
Cleaning	5.00	
Miscellaneous Expenses	15.00	
Debtors	279.50	
Bank Current Account	16,728.52	
Petty Cash	100.00	
Creditors		66.90
VAT Payable		385.57
Capital		15,000.00
	24,662.27	24,662.27

Note:

1   The Debtors' figure is the total of all the balance figures from the Sales
    (Debtors') Ledger.
2   The Creditors' figure is the total of all the balance figures from the Purchases
    (Creditors') Ledger.

5 Bank Reconciliation

A bank reconciliation is a process used to explain the difference between the balance in the bank statement received from the company's bank and the corresponding balance shown in the company's own bank account record. There will usually be differences between the two bank statements.

The differences are usually due to one or more of the following reasons:

- A lodgement made by the company does not appear on the bank statement from the bank.
- A cheque issued by the company has not been presented to the bank and therefore does not appear on the bank statement from the bank.
- An error made by the bank.
- An error made by the company in its own bank account records.

The bank reconciliation process is used to identify the differences in the balances and make adjustments in order to equalise the balance figures. A completed bank reconciliation will result in both the adjusted bank balance (as per the bank statement) and the adjusted balance in the company's bank record (the bank account in the Nominal (General) Ledger) being equal.

> **TASK M-33**
>
> Perform a bank reconciliation using the bank statement on Source Documents, page 20 and the bank account in the Nominal (General) Ledger.

The first step in completing a bank reconciliation is to compare the bank statement with the Cash Receipts Book and the Cash Payments Book and identify any differences between them.

A bank reconciliation is then performed by completing two calculations. The first calculation uses the bank statement and makes adjustments to it as follows:

Balance as per bank statement	€16,750.05
Adjustments: Add deposits not shown on bank statement	+ €0.00
Subtract cheques issued but not shown on bank statement	− €47.38
Subtract any payments recorded in own accounts but not shown on bank statement (e.g. DD or SO)	− €0.00
Adjusted Bank Balance	€16,702.67

The second calculation uses the bank account in the Nominal (General) Ledger and makes adjustments to it as follows:

Balance as per Bank Nominal Ledger	€16,728.52
Adjustments: Add interest earned	+ €0.00
Subtract bank charges	− €25.85
Add/Subtract any errors in Nominal Bank account	+ €0.00
Adjusted Bank Nominal Ledger	€16,702.67

The Bank Reconciliation is complete when the two balance figures are the same.

6 VAT 3 Form

Every company who is registered for VAT must make a return to the Collector General on a two-monthly basis. This is done be completing a VAT 3 form which is sent to each company for the purpose of making a return. The VAT 3 form is pre-printed with all the company information such as name, address, VAT number, etc. The company has simply to calculate the amount of VAT collected and the amount paid out and enter these figures on the form. The amount to be paid to (or in some cases repaid from) the Collector General is then entered on the form.

TASK M-34

Complete a VAT 3 form for the month of January ##.

The necessary information for completing the VAT 3 form can be obtained from the VAT account in the Nominal (General) Ledger. The figures to be entered are as follows:

1   The VAT account is a Credit account, which means that the Balance figure is normally a Credit amount. In this case the Balance figure is the amount of VAT which has to be paid to the Collector General, and is entered in the T3 box on the form.
    However, if the Balance figure is a Debit figure, then the figure will be in brackets and will usually have the letters Dr in the right margin. This amount has to be repaid from the Collector General and is entered in the T4 box on the form.
2   The total VAT collected (VAT output) is the total of the Credit column, and therefore this figure is entered in box T1 on the VAT 3 form.
3   The total VAT paid (VAT input) is the total of the Credit column, and therefore this figure is entered in box T2 on the VAT 3 form.

COMPANY NAME: J.P. MURPHY ELECTRIC

Nominal (General) Ledger   Nominal Account: VAT Payable

Date	Details	F	Dr	Cr	Bal
31/01/##	VAT on Sales (Jan ##)	SDB		1,824.20	1,824.20
31/01/##	VAT on Purchases (Jan ##)	PDB	1,436.75		387.45
31/01/##	VAT on Petty Cash Purchases	PCB	1.88		385.57
			1,438.63	1,824.20	

T2   T1   **T3 if Credit**
T4 if Debit

The completed VAT3 form should look like the following:

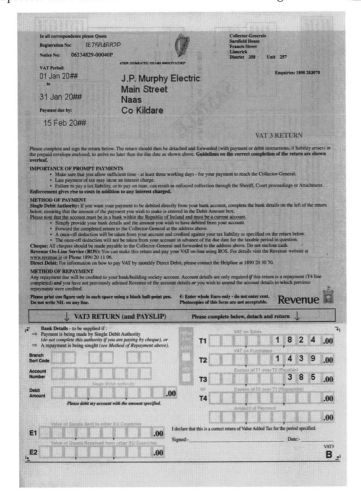

7 Exercises M-1, M-2, M-3 and M-4

Exercise M-1

1 Enter any adjustments needed as a result of the Bank Reconciliation.

2 Write up the source documents on pages 22–58 in the appropriate daybooks.

3 A direct debit of €1532.75 was made for salaries on 28/2/##. Write up this transaction in the appropriate daybook.

4 Cheque number 200207 was cashed on 28/02/## to restore the petty cash imprest to €100.00. Calculate the amount of this cheque and enter it in the appropriate daybook.

5 Total all daybooks and cross-check the totals.

6 Post the entries from all the daybooks to the appropriate ledger accounts.

7 Extract a trial balance as at the last day of February ##.

8 Perform a Bank Reconciliation using the Bank Statement on Source Documents page 59.

9 Complete a VAT 3 form for the months of January and February ##.

Exercise M-2

1 Enter any adjustments needed as a result of the Bank Reconciliation.

2 Write up the Source Documents on pages 63–83 in the appropriate daybooks.

3 Cheque number 200301 was sent to the Collector General on 12/03/## to pay the VAT for January and February. Calculate the amount of this cheque and enter it in he appropriate daybook.

4 Enter the following direct debit payments in the appropriate daybook
 • €345.00 was paid for rent on 28/03/##
 • €1654.25 was made for Salaries on 31/03/##

5 Cheque number 200305 was cashed on 31/03/## to restore the petty cash imprest to €100.00. Calculate the amount of this cheque and enter it in the appropriate daybook.

6 Total all daybooks and cross-check the totals.

7 Post the entries from all the daybooks to the appropriate ledger accounts.

8 Extract a trial balance as at the last day of March ##.

9 Perform a Bank Reconciliation using the Bank Statement on Source Documents page 84.

10 Complete a VAT 3 form for the month of March ##.

Exercise M-3

1 Gem Jewellers, Patrick's Street, Cork, commenced business on 01/01/## with a capital investment of €25,000.00. €24,800.00 of this was deposited in their current bank account and €200.00 was placed in petty cash. Use the General Journal to record these entries.

2 Write up the source documents on pages 93–113 in the appropriate daybooks.

3 Write up the following Direct Debit payments into the appropriate daybook:
   • Rent payment of €450.00 on 25/01/##
   • Salary payment of €1108.56 on 30/01/##

4 Cheque number 215014 was cashed on 31/01/## to restore the petty cash imprest to €200.00. Calculate the amount of this cheque and enter it in the appropriate daybook.

5 Total all daybooks and cross-check the totals.

6 Post the entries from all the daybooks to the appropriate ledger accounts.

7 Extract a trial balance as at the last day of January ##.

8 Perform a Bank Reconciliation using the Bank Statement on Source Documents page 114.

9 Complete a VAT 3 form for the month of January ##.

Exercise M-4

1 Gem Jewellers, Patrick's Street, Cork, invested a further €8,000 of Capital in their business on 01/02/## which was deposited in their current bank account. Use the General Journal to record this entry.

2 Enter any adjustments needed as a result of the Bank Reconciliation.

3 Write up the source documents on pages 120–168 in the appropriate daybooks.

4 Write up the following Direct Debit payments into the appropriate daybook:
   - Rent payment of €465.00 on 26/02/##
   - Salary payment of €1317.84 on 28/02/##

5 Cheque number 215205 was cashed on 28/02/## to restore the petty cash imprest to €200.00. Calculate the amount of this cheque and enter it in the appropriate daybook.

6 Total all daybooks and cross-check the totals.

7 Post the entries from all the daybooks to the appropriate ledger accounts.

8 Extract a trial balance as at the last day of February ##.

9 Perform a Bank Reconciliation using the Bank Statement on Source Documents page 169.

10 Complete a VAT 3 form for the months of January and February ##.

PART 2

Installing the Program and Creating New Company

1 Installing the TASBooks Program and Creating a New Company

When the TASBooks program is installed on a computer, it may have a 'demo' company set up and be ready to perform transactions on that company. The program will also allow you to set up a new company and probably create a new company during installation. In order to perform the tasks set out in this book, it is necessary to set up a new company.

This book sets out transactions for three different companies, but if your program is a single-company version, then it will only be possible to set up one company. The name of this company will probably be the name of your college and cannot be changed. This does not affect the tasks which are set out in this book. However, if your program is a single-user version, then it will be necessary to delete (or 'clear down') the files for the first company and simply change the details, such as address, phone numbers, etc., and continue with the transactions for the next company.

Note:

The pointer symbol [pointer symbol] is used in this book to indicate that you should point to the option indicated after the symbol and click the left mouse button in order to select the option indicated.

Starting TASBooks the First Time

The first time TASBooks is started, it is necessary to activate the program. When the program is started for the first time, the Product Activation Assistant window will be displayed, as shown below:

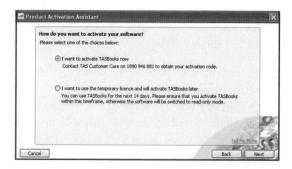

Enter the Serial Number supplied by TAS.

Enter the Company Name. This must be entered exactly as registered with TAS, including punctuation and spaces.

The program may attempt to activate the program automatically if the computer is connected to the Internet. If not, then the following window will be displayed.

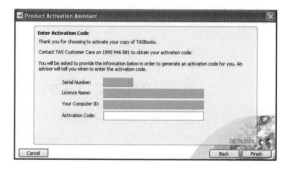

 I want to activate TASBooks now

 Next

The program will then display the following screen with the Serial Number, Licence Name and Your Computer ID already completed. Insert the Activation Code.

 Finish

The following window will then appear with the relevant information
displayed:

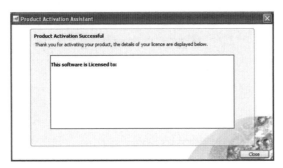

 Close and the following screen will be displayed:

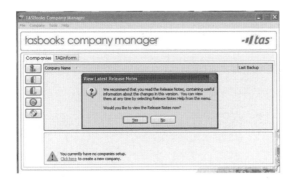

 No

The following screen will then be displayed:

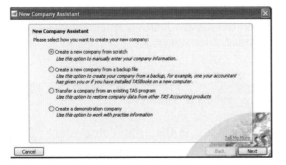

 Create a new company from scratch

 Next

The following screen will then be displayed:

Enter the relevant company information.

 Next

The following screen will then be displayed:

Note:

If you have a single-user licence, then the name will probably be the name of your college and cannot be changed.

 Finish and the company will be created.

 Close when the process is complete.

The new company will appear in the list of companies in the TASBooks Company Manager window.

Note:

A new company may be created at any time from the TASBooks Company Manager window by selecting the Company menu and then New Company.

Cleardown Data

Before it is possible to start inputting data into the company accounts, there are a number of Nominal Accounts, VAT accounts, Bank Accounts, Default accounts and structures that must be set up. When the new company was created, the program created Nominal Accounts, VAT accounts, Bank Accounts and Default accounts automatically. However, it is much better to create these accounts yourself, as the accounts and structures created by the program are not the most suitable for training purposes. We will therefore delete all the accounts and start from scratch using the 'Cleardown Data' function.

The complete process is detailed as follows:

1   **Load the company.** If there is an icon on the desktop for TASBooks, then the program is selected by simply pointing to that icon and double clicking the left mouse button. The TASBooks Company Manager window will be displayed.

If you have just created the company, then this window will already be open:

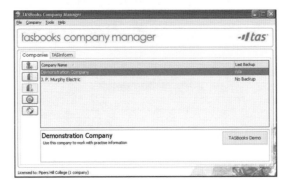

 Company

Point to the company name and click the left mouse button once then **Select** and click the left mouse button. Alternatively, the company may be selected by pointing to the company name and double-clicking the left mouse button. The following TASBooks Company Assistant window will be displayed:

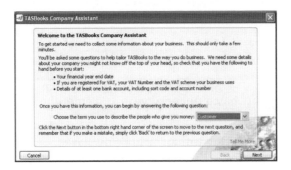

Next

The following window will be displayed:

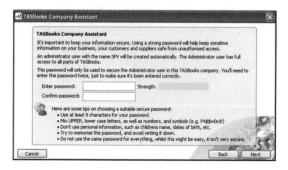

2 **Enter Password and Basic Information**
Enter a password in the 'Enter password' field
Enter the same password in the 'Confirm password' field.
This will be the administrator (Supervisor) password for the **SPV** user.

 Next and the following window will be displayed:

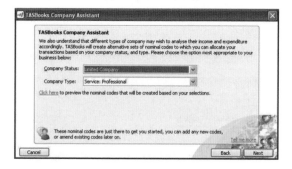

 Next and the following window will be displayed.

 I want a monthly based financial year, and enter the starting month and year

 Next and the following window will be displayed:

Enter the VAT Registration Number.

Next and the following window will be displayed:

Next and the following window will be displayed:

Select the Deposit Account and the TPS Clearing A/C and Delete.

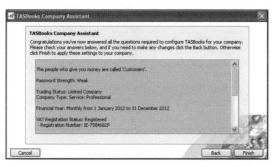

Next and the following window will be displayed:

Finish and the basic data for the company will be set up. A window telling you that the company is now ready for use will be displayed.

Close

3 **Log in to the company**. When the company is selected, the Login Screen will be displayed as shown below:

Enter the User Code and **Password**

Login

A number of information windows will be displayed when you Login. Shut down these windows each time they appear.

4 **Cleardown Data Files.** This task removes all the data from the company which the program has just created and will allow you to create the company exactly as you require. This task is accomplished as follows:

0 Central

4 User Password Maintenance

9 Cleardown Data Files

The following screen will then be displayed:

 **All Data** (the dot will appear in the All Data selection)

Cleardown

The program will then display the following warning message:

 **Yes** and the program will display the following progress window:

When the process is complete the following window will be displayed:

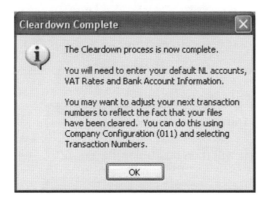

OK and the cleardown is complete.

5 **Set up new user**. This task creates another user with a separate password that may be used by other users of this company. These users may have full or limited rights with regard to updating the company files. A new user is set up as follows:

0 Central

4 User Password Maintenance

1 Maintain Users

The User Manager screen will appear:

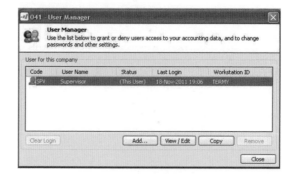

▶ **Add...**

The following screen may then be displayed:

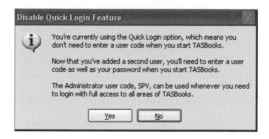

▶ **Yes**

The following screen for the input of the new user details will then be displayed:

Type the User Code and the Name for this user. Then set the password:

▶ **Set Password**

The following screen will then be displayed:

Enter a password in the 'Enter password' field
Enter the same password in the 'Confirm password' field

 OK and ⬆ Yes and the new user will be saved.

Close the User Manager window.

6   **Renumber Suspense Account**. When the data file cleardown took place, the program left one nominal account. This account is 2500 Suspense Account. The first thing we will do is renumber this as **9999 Suspense Account** as follows.

⬆ **0 Central**

⬆ **5 General Operations / Utilities**

⬆ **3 Change Nominal Account Number**

The Change Nominal Account screen will then be displayed with the following warning message:

⬆ OK and the warning will disappear.

⬆ the label in the Current Account Details (the words 'Account Number' in blue underlined text) and the list of Nominal Accounts will be displayed. At this stage there will only be one account in the list (2500), so select this account.

Enter the number **9999** in the Account Number field of the New Account Details

The screen should then look like the following:

 **Change** and then **OK** and the renumbering will be complete.

Close the Change Nominal Account window.

7 **Create Nominal Account Groups.** When nominal accounts are being created they are normally grouped together into the various nominal groups, namely Income, Expense, Asset, Liability and Owner Equity. There may be more groups if required, but these are sufficient for our purposes. There is a Default group already created, but if all accounts are grouped into a Default group, it will create errors when entering some new products.

Nominal account groups are created as follows:

 **1 Nominal**

 **1 Nominal Accounts**

 **3 Maintain Nominal Groups**

The program will present a screen for the input of the following information for each nominal group:

GROUP   Type the group name (INCOME, EXPENSE, ASSET, LIABILITY and OWNER EQ.)

Description   Type a description for each group (Income Group, Expense Group, Asset Group, Liability Group, Owner Equity Group)

When the first group has been entered, the screen should look like the following:

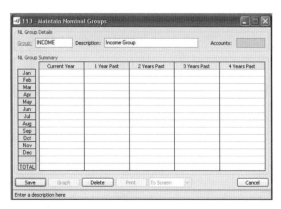

 Save and then Yes to confirm to save the nominal account group each time.

8 **Create the Nominal Accounts** listed in the table below. Some of these accounts are required as default accounts in order to set up a company. The other accounts are required in order to carry out the tasks set for J.P. Murphy Electric in this book, and are generally some of the accounts required by all companies.

The accounts shown are the default accounts that must be set up when creating a new company. These accounts have special significance to the TASBooks program and if they are not set up, the program will display a warning message when you are logging into the company.

Account **9999 Suspense Account** will already be set up, as this is the account which was renumbered in a previous step. This account is also a default account.

At this stage, it is only necessary to create Nominal accounts for other companies as the other accounts will be created as part of a later exercise for those companies.

The details on how to set up Nominal accounts are contained on page 134.

NOMINAL ACCOUNTS					
Number	Description	Type	Nominal Group	Analysis Category	Dr or Cr
1000	Sales	Income	Income	Income	Cr
2000	Purchases	Expense	Expense	Expenses	Dr
3999	Unused Default	Expense	Expense	Expenses	Dr
7000	Debtors	Asset	Asset	Debtors	Dr
7100	Stock	Asset	Asset	Other Current Asset	Dr
7200	Bank Current A/C	Asset	Asset	Other Current Asset	Dr
7300	Petty Cash	Asset	Asset	Other Current Asset	Dr
8000	Creditors	Liability	Liability	Creditors	Cr
8100	VAT Payable	Liability	Liability	Other Current Liab	Cr
8200	PAYE/PRSI Payable	Liability	Liability	Other Current Liab	Cr
9100	Retained Profit	Owner's Equity	Owner Eq	Owner's Equity	Cr
9200	Profit Balance B/F	Owner's Equity	Owner Eq	Owner's Equity	Cr
9999	Suspense Account	Owner's Equity	Owner Eq	Owner's Equity	Cr

9 **Set Up VAT Rates.** This task is accomplished as follows:

▶ **0 Central**

▶ **3 VAT Rates and Reporting**

▶ **1 Maintain VAT Rates**

When you select this last option, the following warning will appear:

This System Maintenance Program warning appears each time you select a maintenance option. ▶ **OK** to continue.

A screen for the input of VAT rates will be displayed. Because VAT rates change over time, this book uses the following sample VAT rates. These may not be the same as the current rates, but all the tasks in this book have been designed for use these rates.

Input the following VAT rates and percentages:

Code	Rate	Acct	Dept	NL Description	Short Description	R/N	Rate Type
1	20%	8100	100	VAT Payable	20% Resale	R	Standard
2	12.5%	8100	100	VAT Payable	12.5% Resale	R	Lower
3	0%	8100	100	VAT Payable	0% Resale	R	Zero
4	0%	8100	100	VAT Payable	Exempt Resale	R	Exempt
5	20%	8100	100	VAT Payable	20% Non-Resale	N	Standard
6	12.5%	8100	100	VAT Payable	12.5% Non-Resale	N	Lower
7	0%	8100	100	VAT Payable	0% Non-Resale	N	Zero
8	0%	8100	100	VAT Payable	Exempt Non-Resale	N	Exempt
9	0%	8100	100	VAT Payable	Outside Scope Rate	N	None

In each case simply type the **Rate**, **Acct**, **Short Description**, **R** or **N** for Resale or Non Resale, and select a **Rate Type** from the list by clicking the arrow. The program will complete the rest for each rate as it is entered.

When the rates are entered there are five default rates that must be selected. These are:

Default Standard Rate	(1 – 20% Resale)
Default Lower Rate	(2 – 12.5% Resale)
Default Zero Rate	(7 – 0% Non-Resale)
Default Exempt Rate	(4 – Exempt Resale)
Outside Scope Rate	(9 – Outside Scope Rate, used where there is no VAT on a transaction)

Select the appropriate rate in each case as follows:

beside the field for the rate to be selected. The nine rates will be displayed in a drop down menu. **Point to the rate required** and click the left mouse button.

When this task is completed the screen should look like the following:

Save and the VAT rates and percentages will be set up for this company.

10 **Set Up Bank Accounts**. Bank accounts are set up as follows:

4 Cash Book

1 Bank Accounts

1 Maintain Bank Accounts

This System Configuration Program warning appears again.

OK to continue and the following screen will be displayed:

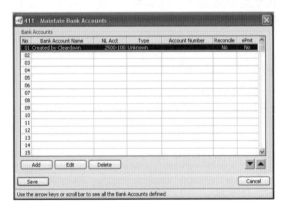

Delete the Bank Account created at cleardown and  **Add** and the following window will be displayed:

Enter the following Bank Accounts:

No	Description	Nominal Account		Reconcile	Account Type
1	Bank Current A/C	7200	-100	Y	Current Account
2	Petty Cash	7300	-100	N	Other

Enter the Bank Account Name, the bank account Nominal Ledger number, tick Yes or No if the account is to be reconciled or not, and select an account type. (The current account will be reconciled, and the petty cash will not be reconciled, as there will be no bank statement for petty cash).

When the bank accounts have been entered the screen will look like the following:

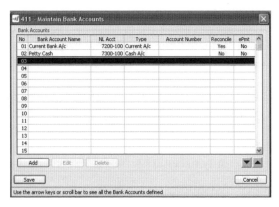

 **Save** and the Bank Accounts will be set up for this company.

11 **Enter TASBooks Configuration Data**. The basic information for this company was entered during the creation of the company. The remaining information, however, which is necessary to allow transactions to be entered into the company accounts must now be entered. There are a number of accounts and options that must be set up in the various ledgers. These are set up as follows:

▶ **0 Central**

▶ **1 General Company Information**

▶ **2 TASBooks Configuration**

This System Configuration Program warning appears.

▶ OK to continue.
The program then presents the following screen:

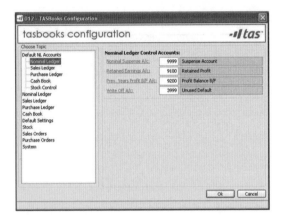

This screen allows for the input of the various Nominal accounts required by the program. It is necessary to select the section on the left-hand side, 'Choose Topic' section and select the nominal account on the right-hand side. There are a number of default options which we will not be using so we will select the Nominal Account '3999' as the Nominal account in such cases.

Select the sections which follow in the 'Choose Topic' section and the Nominal accounts which are required will appear on the right-hand side, Select the Nominal account by pointing to the label in blue underlined text and clicking the left mouse button. The list of Nominal accounts will be displayed and it is then only necessary to select the accounts shown below.

▶ **Default NL Accounts**

▶ **Nominal Ledger**

Nominal Ledger Control Accounts

Nominal Suspense A/C:	9999
Retained Earnings A/C:	9100
Prev. Years Profit B/F A/C:	9200
Write-Off A/c:	3999

Default NL Accounts

Sales Ledger

Default Sales Ledger Accounts

Debtors' A/C (Customers):	7000
Sales A/C:	1000
Discounts Given:	3999

Sales Ledger Receipt Adjustment Accounts

Bank Charges:	3999
Write-Offs (Under Pmt):	3999
Write-Backs (Over Pmt):	3999
Currency Gain/Loss:	3999
Other Gain/Loss:	3999

 Default NL Accounts

 Purchase Ledger

Purchase Ledger Accounts

Creditors' A/C (Suppliers):	8000
Discounts Received:	3999

Purchase Ledger Payment Adjustment Options

Bank Charges:	3999
Write-Backs (Under Pmt):	3999
Write-Offs (Over Pmt):	3999
Currency Gain/Loss:	3999
Other Gain/Loss:	3999

 Default NL Accounts

 Cash Book

Bank Interest and Charges Accounts

Interest Received:	3999
Interest Paid:	3999
Bank Charges:	3999
Cheque Book Duty:	3999

 Default NL Accounts

 Stock Control

Stock Accounts

Cost of Sales:	2000
Stock:	7100
Stock Adjustments:	7100

Sales Ledger

 Overdue Options

Nominal Ledger Account

Interest Charged A/C: 3999

 Sales Ledger

 Receipt Allocation

Sales Ledger Receipt Allocation

Select 'Manual Allocation' from the options offered in the Default Method field.

 Purchase Ledger

 Payment Allocation

Purchase Ledger Payment Allocation

Select 'Manual Allocation' from the options offered in the Default Method field.

 Stock

 Stock Control

N.B.   Make sure the you tick the box 'Select the above option, without prompting the user' as shown below:

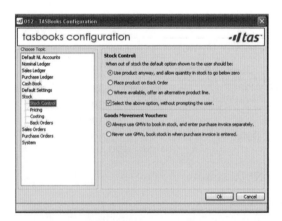

Since we will not be dealing with stock control or stock movements, we wish the program to ignore the stock quantities when entering transactions.

Note:

Failure to set this configuration will lead to great difficulties when entering products and sales orders.

 Sales Orders

 Entry / Printing Options

N.B. Make sure the you tick the box:
"Allow user to print Sales Order from 611 – Enter / Edit Sales Orders" as shown below:

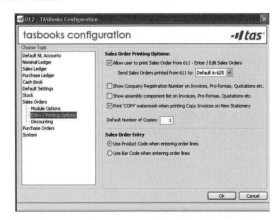

Setting this option will cause the program to prompt the user to print and post Sales Orders when saving them. If this option is not set, then the user will have to remember to print and post each sales order.

 Purchase Orders

 Entry / Costing Options

Goods Movement Accrual Account
GMV Accrual Account: 3999

When all the above configurations have been set, OK and then Yes to confirm and save, and all the configuration information will be saved.

Note:

The set-up of a blank company is now complete. At this stage it is possible to store or back up the files for this company before any transactions have been entered, and then transfer or restore them in order to work on this company again, or to perform the tasks on the other companies in this book.

Storing or backing up the files at this stage saves having to set up each company from scratch each time.

Create Additional Accounts and Products to Start J.P. Murphy Electric

In order to carry out the tasks set out in this book for J.P. Murphy Electric, it is necessary to set up the following additional accounts, customers, suppliers and products:

1 **Set the Nominal, Sales and Purchase Ledger Dates** to 31/01/20## as described on page 134. This sets the posting dates to the last day of the month and is preferable for training purposes.
2 **Set up** the additional **Nominal accounts** listed below. The details on how to set up Nominal accounts are contained on page 134.

Number	Description	Type	Nominal Group	Analysis Category	Dr or Cr
1100	Repairs Income	Income	Income	Income	Cr
3100	Rent	Expense	Expense	Expenses	Dr
3300	Telephone	Expense	Expense	Expenses	Dr
3400	Post	Expense	Expense	Expenses	Dr
3500	Stationery	Expense	Expense	Expenses	Dr
3600	Cleaning	Expense	Expense	Expenses	Dr
3700	Miscellaneous Expenses	Expense	Expense	Expenses	Dr
9000	Capital	Owners Equity	Owner Equity	Owners Equity	Cr

3 **Set up Customer Standing Data** from the customer details shown below. The procedure for maintaining customer standing data is detailed on page 139.

Code	M001
Name	James Mahon
Address	Willow View
	Prosperous
	Co Kildare

Code	E001
Name	The Electrical Shop
Address	The Mill
	Celbridge
	Co Kildare

Code	N001
Name	New Age Contractors
Address	Main Street
	Kilcullen
	Co Kildare

Code	C001
Name	Cash Sale
Address	

Code	T001
Name	Tomorrow's Electronics
Address	Main Street
	Naas
	Co Kildare

4 **Set up Suppliers' Standing Data** from the supplier details shown below.
The procedure for maintaining suppliers' standing data is detailed on page
139.

Code	S101
Name	Solon International
Address	Unit 12 Sunshine Ind Est
	Crumlin Rd
	Dublin 12

Code	P101
Name	Philem Ireland
Address	Unit 126
	Kenilworth Place
	Dublin 8

Code	M101
Name	Modern Communications
Address	City West Park
	Naas Road
	Co Dublin

5   **Enter Products** from the product details shown below. The procedure for maintaining product details is detailed on page 144.

Code	Description	VAT Rate	Retail Price
T114	14" Solon TV	1–21%	€189.00
T116	16" Solon TV	1–21%	€229.00
D101	Philem DVD Player	1–21%	€245.00
R100	Repairs	2–12.5%	€14.80

Note:

Ensure that the item 'R100 – Repairs' is entered as VAT rate '2 – 12.5%' and as Sales Account '1100 – Repairs Income' instead of '1000 – Sales'.

Installing a Company on Multiple Machines

The process of setting up the same company on a number of machines can be simplified by following the procedure detailed below:

1   Install the program on all machines. Ensure that you install the program in the same way on all machines. Use the same folder for the program in each case. Follow the procedure on pages 67–69.
2   Create the company on each machine. Follow the procedure for creating the company as detailed on pages 69–70 for each machine. Ensure that you use the same name and folder for the new company on each machine.
3   Set up the company on ONE machine only. Follow the procedure on pages 71–87.
4   Backup the data files only from the company that has been set up. The procedure for performing this task is detailed on page 158–159.
5   Restore the back-up files to each machine as detailed below on page 160–162.

Setting Up a Company – Summary

The following is a summary of all the steps detailed elsewhere in this book. Eventually you will only need this page to set up a new company.

The column labelled Menu is the three-digit number which is used to select that particular option in the TASBooks Accounting Plus program. This option may be selected by holding down the Alt key and pressing each digit using the numbers on the top row of the keyboard.

The column labelled Page Ref is the page number in this book where the full details of each operation may be found.

Step	Menu	Operation	Page Ref
1		Install the TASBooks Program	67
2		Create New Company	69
3	049	Cleardown Data Files	74
4	041	Enter New User Code and Password (Optional)	76
5	053	Renumber Suspense Account	77
6	113	Create Nominal Groups	78
7	111	Create Nominal Accounts	79
8	131	Print Nominal Accounts (Optional)	79
9	031	Set Up VAT Rates	80
10	411	Set Up Bank Accounts	82
11	012	Enter TASBooks Configuration Data	84
12		Create additional Accounts, Products, etc., for J.P. Murphy	88
13		Back Up Data Files	158
14		Restore to other machines if required	160

Note:

The company name may not be J.P. Murphy Electric, but the college name or the
name of the new company that has been set up.

PART 3

Computerised Bookkeeping

1 Computerised Bookkeeping

Computerised bookkeeping/accounts programs (packages) make the running of a business very simple by providing a straightforward method of recording all transactions that affect the business. Computerised bookkeeping will do everything that can be done using a manual system of bookkeeping, and in effect, a bookkeeping program is just a manual system transferred to a computer. Using a bookkeeping program saves time and money and eliminates repetition while maintaining the integrity of the accounts. For example, entering a single sales invoice will update the sales daybook and will automatically update the customer's account, the debtors' control account, sales account and the VAT account, along with the profit and loss account and balance sheet. This all happens automatically, provided that the data is entered correctly, and there is no need to worry about the knock-on effects.

The notes in this chapter are written in a very practical manner. Each task is set out separately, and step-by-step instructions are given on how to perform that task. The tasks follow the same sequence as in the manual bookkeeping section, with the same source documents being used for both manual and computerised. This means that manual and computerised books may be compared at all stages. It will be very helpful to compare the output from the computer program with the manual daybooks and ledgers at regular intervals, as this will enhance the understanding of both systems of bookkeeping.

The disadvantage of following the sequence of tasks as laid out here is that we will not be covering each section of the computer program individually, but rather, we will be jumping from one section to another in order to carry out each required task. That said, the summary section will assist you in locating the page on how to perform each task later. Use the contents page to locate the relevant instructions for performing any task throughout the book.

We have used directions and screenshots from the TASBooks program for the purposes of this book, but the tasks and source documents are designed to be used with any computerised accounting program, and the data to be input will be the same no matter what program is being used. The screens displayed by another program may appear different, but there should be no difficulty in performing each task.

The tasks in this section start with the assumption that the bookkeeping/ accounting program is installed on the computer and that the company 'J.P. Murphy Electric' has been created.

Detailed instructions for installing TASBooks program and for creating the company J.P. Murphy Electric are contained in the previous chapter.

Computerised Program: TASBooks Accounting Plus

The following are some general notes on bookkeeping and on the TASBooks program, such as how to select the program on a computer, how to select the correct section, how to move from field to field, etc. Some of these notes are also applicable to other programs.

Note:

The pointer symbol ![pointer] is used in this book to indicate that you should point to the option indicated after the symbol and click the left mouse button in order to select the option indicated.

For example, if you were being asked to select the Sales menu, the notes would read:

![pointer] 2 Sales This means that you should point to '2 Sales' on the menu bar at the top of the screen with the mouse pointer and click the left mouse button.

The ![pointer] symbol will be used extensively throughout this book.

Fields

All data contained in computerised accounting programs is stored in fields. Each field (or box) contains one piece of data. When particular data, such as a customer's account code, is entered into a record, it is stored as a 'key field'. This means that the data in this field can be used to search for particular records, even if you do not know the full code. There are a number of key fields used by TASBooks Accounting Plus. Each key field will be recognised because it is displayed in bold print. There will be a key field at least once in every record.

Note:

1   One very important key is Tab (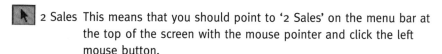). Pressing this key moves the cursor from one field (box) to the next. This is the method used to enter the data in a field and move on to the next field, when inputting data into the computer.
2   Some fields, such as the address, will have a number of lines in the same field. In such cases the Enter key is used to move from one line to the next line within the same field.

Some fields display a selection icon (▼) on the right-hand side of the field. When this icon is beside a field, it means that you must select one of the options displayed in the drop-down menu that appears when you click on this button. It is often possible to select the option required by typing the first letter of the option. The program then recognises this as one of the possible options and displays that option, which can then be accepted by pressing the Tab key, which will select the option and move onto the next field.

Each entry in the computerised program requires at least one date. Where a date is required, the program will normally display the ledger date, and it is only necessary to type the two day-digits in order to enter the full date. Leading zeros are used where there are single figures, e.g. the sixth day of the month would be typed as 06.

Some field labels are displayed in _blue, underlined text_, which indicates a key field and allows the look-up facility to be used. Pointing to the blue, underlined text and clicking the left mouse button will cause the program to display a list of appropriate entries for that field.

Function Keys

The function keys, F1–F10, on the top row of the keyboard are used to perform special tasks. Some of these functions are also available as buttons, at the bottom-left corner of the screen. The functions are operated by simply pressing the appropriate function key, or by pointing to the appropriate function button and clicking the left mouse button.

The functions available using these keys are as follows:

KEY	FUNCTION
F1	Displays a help screen
F2	Selects the look-up function for key fields
F3	Clears the record which is on screen
F4	Deletes the record on screen
F5	Finds the first record in the file
F6	Finds the last record in the file
F7	Finds the previous record to the one on screen
F8	Finds the next record to the one on screen
F9	Finds the nearest record to what has been entered in a key field
F10	Saves the record on screen to file

On-screen Instructions

Each time the program requires you to enter data or perform a certain task, it will prompt you with a simple instruction. These instructions appear at the bottom of the screen.

Double Entry

Bookkeeping programs use a double-entry system for the entry of all amounts into the accounts system. This is a standard method used in accounting and there are many fine books written to explain it. However, as far as you are concerned, you must adopt the rule that every entry in the system must have an amount or amounts in the Debit column and an amount or amounts in the Credit column. The totals of both columns must match exactly to the last cent in order for the entry to be valid. The number of entries in both columns does not matter, as long as the totals are the same. This will be explained further when we are posting to the ledgers and when entering source documents into the computer program.

Selecting the TASBooks program

The program is started in the normal way as follows:

- Shortcut
  If there is an icon on the screen for TASBooks, then the program is selected by simply pointing to that icon and double clicking the left mouse button.
- Start Button
  If there is no TASBooks icon on the screen, then the program may be selected from the Start menu in the normal way. The TASBooks launcher will be in the TAS folder.

Once the program has been selected it will load and automatically display the TASBooks Company Manager window. The TASBooks Company Manager window will list the companies available on your computer.

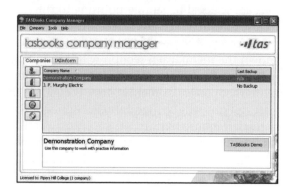

Point to the company required and click the left mouse button. Then point to the Start TASBooks button and click the left mouse button again. Alternatively you may point to the company required and double-click the left mouse button.

Entering the TASBooks Program

Once you select the required company, the following log-in screen will be displayed:

Because accounting programs contain a great deal of sensitive information, the program should be protected by a User Code and a Password.

Type the correct User Code, which will be given to you, and press the Tab key.

Type the correct Password, which will be given to you, and click **Login** or press the Enter key.

Selecting the Correct Section

The TASBooks program has a number of different sections, which are listed as menus on the menu bar at the top of the screen, as shown below:

The various sections are selected by simply pointing to the required icon and clicking the left mouse button. Once you select one of the sections listed above, a drop-down menu will appear under the menu selected. When you move the mouse down the menu, each section will be highlighted, and a second, sub-menu will appear. This sub-menu lists the individual options available from within that particular menu. Move the mouse into the sub-menu area and these options will be highlighted. Highlight the option required and click the left mouse button.

There are a number of functions that are available as icons on the toolbar. If the option required is on the toolbar, then it a simple matter of pointing to the icon and clicking the left mouse button.

Note:

> If the toolbar is not displayed, then it can be activated by pointing to the menu bar, clicking the *right* mouse button and selecting 'Toolbar' from the drop-down menu.

All options are run by selecting from three menus or by clicking an icon on the toolbar. For example, in order to print the sales and cash daybooks, the correct option is selected as follows:

2 Sales   (the Sales menu will appear on screen)

1 Customers   (the Customer's sub-menu will appear)

2 Customer Account Enquiry   (the Maintain Customers screen will appear)

When this selection is made, the following window will appear:

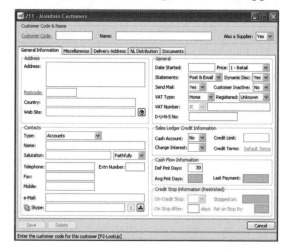

You will notice that this screen is titled **212 – Maintain Customers**. The number **212** is derived from the individual numbers selected in order to select this particular option (see above), thus producing a three-digit number.

All options have a three-digit number, and as you use the program, you will begin to remember the three-digit number associated with particular options. Once you know the number, you may find it quicker to select that option by holding down the Alt key and typing the three-digit number. (The menus will appear as you type the numbers, and the option chosen will appear as soon as you type the last digit.)

Customising the Company

In a classroom situation in which each student is usually working with the same companies, it is difficult to distinguish one student's company from another's. In such cases, it is very useful to amend the company name to include the student's name or initials. This also helps in the identification of printouts, as the company name (as amended) will appear on each of the printouts.

This option of amending the company name is only possible if the program has a multi-company licence and is accomplished as follows:

0 Central

1 General Company Information

1 Company Configuration

The program will then display the Maintain Company Information screen, and will display a message informing you that a lock has been placed on some of the company files, as shown below:

> **System Configuration Program** ✕
>
> ⚠ Whilst using this program many features will be unavailable to other users. We recommend that no other user accesses this company data until you have finished.
>
> OK

OK to continue.

The screen for the input of the company general information will be displayed. Use the mouse to place the cursor beside the name 'J.P. Murphy' and click the left mouse button twice – but slowly (you must perform two separate clicks in order to place the cursor after the company name). Enter your name or initials in brackets after the company name. When you have completed this task the screen should look like the following:

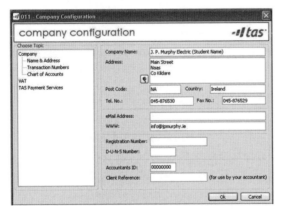

Save and the company name will be changed. The new name will appear on all printouts, but will not appear on the top line of the program until you log out and log in to the company again.

Reports

There are a great number of reports that may be obtained from a computerised bookkeeping program. Running these reports causes the program to search the company files and assemble the required information in an understandable format. The running of any of these reports does not update the files and they can therefore be run as often as required.

The program defines how the reports are presented, so it is only necessary to select the report required and input some simple selections. Each report will provide prompts with the most likely options and, generally, it is only necessary to press the Tab key to accept the options offered. The prompt line at the bottom of the screen will provide instructions with what to input each time a piece of data is required.

Most reports require the input of the Starting and Ending Periods or the Starting and Ending Dates for the report. When inputting Starting and Ending periods (months) it must be remembered that Period 1 is the first period of the financial year of the company. This can be any month of the year, so it is not necessarily January. The period numbers are counted from the first month of the financial year.

Exiting the TASBooks Program

At the end of each session, you must exit the program correctly. Before attempting to exit the program, make sure all that all TASBooks windows are closed. The program is exited as follows:

 File

Exit TASBooks

or

 **Close Program Button**

The program will then display a window asking you if you want to exit TASBooks.

Yes and the program will shut down.

Closing the TASBooks Company Manager Window

When you selected the company that you were using, the TASBooks Company Manager window minimised itself, and is still displayed on the taskbar. This window must also be closed as follows:

 TASBooks Company Manger icon on the taskbar.

(The TASBooks Company Manger window will reappear on screen)

File

Exit

or

 **Close Program Button**

Interactive Flowcharts

One very useful feature of the TASBooks program is the flowchart option, which may be used with certain sections of the program. This is a graphical interface that allows the user to select the required option from a flowchart.

Customers Interactive Flowchart

This flowchart is selected as follows:

 2 Sales

 **1 Customers**

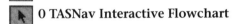 **0 TASNav Interactive Flowchart**

When this option is selected the following window will be displayed:

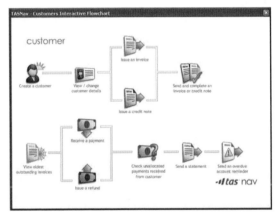

The required option is selected by simply pointing to the required option and clicking the left mouse button.

Suppliers Interactive Flowchart

This flowchart is selected as follows:

3 Purchases

1 Suppliers

0 TASNav Interactive Flowchart

When this option is selected the following window will be displayed:

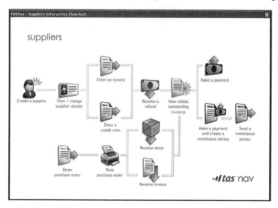

The required option is selected by simply pointing to the required option and clicking the left mouse button.

Cash Book Interactive Flowchart

This flowchart is selected as follows:

4 Cash Book

1 Bank Accounts

0 TASNav Interactive Flowchart

When this option is selected the following window will be displayed:

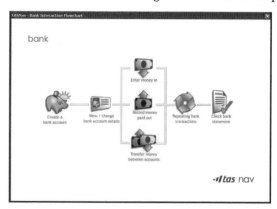

The required option is selected by simply pointing to the required option and clicking the left mouse button.

Products Interactive Flowchart

This flowchart is selected as follows:

 5 Stock

 1 Products and Services

 0 TASNav Interactive Flowchart

When this option is selected the following window will be displayed:

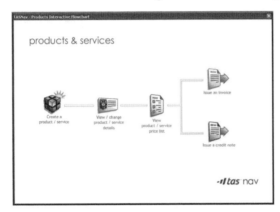

The required option is selected by simply pointing to the required option and clicking the left mouse button.

2 Sales Invoices and Credit Notes

We will begin our work on the computer in the same place as we did in the manual bookkeeping section. In order to begin with this first task, the company J.P. Murphy Electric must already be set up on your computer and some products, customers and suppliers already entered.

Note:

Details on setting up this company are contained in Chapter 1 of Part 2.

TASK C-1

Produce an Invoice from the details of the first invoice on Source Documents page 2.

The procedure of producing an Invoice is twofold. Firstly the customer and product details must be entered on a Sales Order. The Sales Order is then printed and posted in order to produce the Invoice and post the details to the correct Daybook and Ledgers.

Enter Sales Order

This option is used to create sales Invoices, Credit Notes, Quotations, etc., by entering the customer details and the details of products/services to be supplied. This option is selected as follows:

 6 Sales Orders

 1 Sales Orders   *or*   Sales Orders

 1 Enter / Change Sales Orders / Credit Notes

The program then presents a screen for the input of the sales order details.
    The information to be entered is as follows:

Invoice To:	Enter the Customer Code for this invoice and then press the Tab key. (Click the 'Invoice To:' field name or press the F2 function key to display a list of customers.)
Deliver To:	This field is for the selection of a delivery address, which has been input with the customer details. Press the Tab key to skip this field and move to the next field.
Order No.:	This field is used for retrieving existing orders that have not been printed and posted. Orders are retrieved by skipping the 'Invoice To' field and inputting an existing Order Number. The order will be displayed and may then be edited or deleted, provided it has not been processed, as described later.
Date:	Type the date for this order.
Type:	Select, Quotation, Pro-Forma Sales Order or Credit Order by 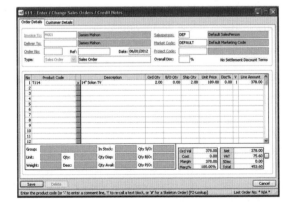, selecting the icon and then selecting the option required. (The Sales Order will be displayed automatically, so press the Tab key to accept the Sales Order and move to the next field.
Ref:	Used for the input of Customer Order Numbers, where they are used.

Accept defaults for the other fields by pressing the Tab key to move onto the next field, until the cursor appears in the Product Code field.

Product Code:	Type the Product Code for each item and the details for that item will be displayed. (Pressing the F2 function key will display a list of products.)
Qty:	Type the number of this product to be invoiced.

Press the Tab key to accept the default values in the remaining fields until the cursor appears in the next Product Code field.

When you have entered the required details the screen should look like the following:

Save to save this order. You may use the F10 function key to save.

The program will request confirmation to save this Sales Order.

 Yes to confirm to save this Sales Order.

Print and Post

The program will then display the following window:

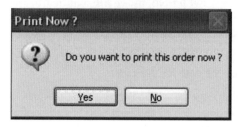

Note:

The 'Print Now?' option will appear provided that the option to 'Allow user to print Sales Order from 611 – Enter / Edit Sales Orders' has been set when configuring TASBooks as described on page 87.

 Yes and the Sales Order will be printed and posted.

Note:

If the Print and Post option is not set in the TASBooks configuration, then each Sales Order must be printed and posted manually by following these steps:

 6 Sales Orders

 2 Print and Post

 5 Print Sales Invoices / Credit Notes

and selecting **Print** in the window which appears.

When the sales order is printed and posted, the program will generate an Invoice Number automatically, which will then be used in processing this order. The Invoice Number can be seen in the Sales Daybook report and may be used to recall this order.

TASK C-2

Produce Invoices from the details of the remaining invoices on page 2.
(Remember to enter and allocate the receipt of the money for the Cash Sale.)

TASK C-3

Produce a Credit Note from the details of the Credit Note on page 2.
(Remember to allocate the Credit Note against the relevant Invoice.)

The production of a Credit Note is exactly the same as an invoice with the exception that you select Credit Note when entering the Sales Order instead of an Invoice.

The program will display the following window asking if you wish to update the stock figures. Select No, as we are not dealing with stock.

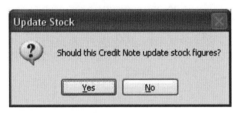

Note:

When you print and post a Credit Note, it will be credited to the customer's account in the Sales Ledger but will not be allocated against the invoice. It is therefore necessary to allocate the Credit Note as will be described later.

TASK C-4 (OPTIONAL)

Display Sales Invoice number 100001 on screen.

Sales Order Enquiry

This option allows the details of any Sales Order to be displayed on screen and/or on hard copy.

This option is selected as follows:

 6 Sales Orders

 1 Sales Orders

 2 Sales Order Enquiry

The program then displays a screen for the input of the Customer Code or the Order Number. The data to be input is as follows:

Customer Code:	If you know the Customer Code for the Sales Order required, enter it here. Press the Tab key to skip this field.
Sales Order Number:	Enter the Sales Order Number. (If you do not know the Sales Order Number you may click on the blue, underlined field name, or use the F2 function key to obtain a list of Sales Orders. If you have entered a Customer Code then the Sales Orders for that customer only will be displayed when you press the F2 key.)
Sales Invoice Number:	Enter the Sales Invoice Number. (If you do not know the Sales Invoice Number you may click on the blue, underlined field name, or use the F2 function key to obtain a list of sales invoices. If you have entered a Customer Code then the Sales Orders for that customer only will be displayed.)
Include Address:	Tick this box by pointing to it and clicking the left mouse button if you wish to have the customer's address included in the output.
Screen:	This field indicates that the enquiry is being sent to the screen.

When the data is entered the screen should look like the following:

 **Print** and the invoice details will be displayed on the screen. The report may be sent to the printer by simply **Print Icon** in the top left-hand corner of the screen display and the output will be sent to the printer to produce a hard copy.

TASK C-5 (OPTIONAL)

Recall Sales Order Number 100003.

Any Sales Order may be recalled at any time. If the Sales Order has been printed and posted, then it may be viewed, but no alterations may be made.

Recalling a Sales Order

A Sales Order may be recalled as follows:

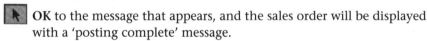 **6 Sales Orders**

1 Sales Orders

1 Enter / Change Invoices / Cr Notes

The Enter / Change Invoices / Cr Notes screen will be displayed. This is the same screen that was used to enter the order.

Press the Tab key to move directly to the **Order No** field.

Type the Sales Order Number required and then press the Tab key. (Remember you may click on the blue, underlined field name or use the F2 function key to display a list of orders).

If the Sales Order has been printed and posted, then a message informing you that you cannot make changes will appear. The order may be examined but no changes may be made to it.

OK to the message that appears, and the sales order will be displayed with a 'posting complete' message.

3 Sales Ledger

The Sales Ledger is used to store all the information relating to customers. All invoices, credit notes and receipts are recorded in the sales ledger. When an invoice or credit note is created using the Sales Order section of the program, it is automatically recorded in the Sales Ledger.

Sales Daybooks

There are a great number of reports available from the computer program. Some of these reports are very similar to the Daybooks and Ledgers produced manually. There are also a number of extra reports that provide information not readily available from the manual system.

> **TASK C-6**
>
> Produce a Sales Daybook report and compare this with your Sales/Sales Returns daybook produced manually for January.

The Sales Daybook report will produce a list of sales invoices and credit notes similar to the Sales Daybook produced manually.

The Sales Daybook is produced as follows:

 2 Sales

 4 Sales Ledger Reports　　　　*or*　　　　

 1 Print Sales / Cash Daybooks

When this option is selected the following screen will be displayed:

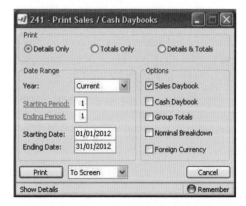

This report is actually two reports in one. It will produce a Sales Daybook and a Cash Daybook. The Cash Daybook shown here is only a record of customer receipts and is not a Cash Receipts (Bank Lodgement) report.

In this case, the periods and dates for the report are correct. The tick for Cash Daybook should be removed in order to display the Sales Daybook only.

 Print and the Sales Daybook report will be displayed on screen. It may be a good idea to compare this report with the Sales/Sales Returns Daybook produced manually.

A hard copy of the report may be printed by simply **Print Icon** 🖨 in the top left-hand corner of the screen display.

Enter and Allocate Cash Received for Cash Sale

TASK C-7

Enter and Allocate the cash received for the Cash Sale Invoice. (The amount of the receipt was €49.95 and the Lodgement Slip Number was 101.)

Every time an invoice is processed for a cash sale, the money received at the time of sale must be entered and allocated in the Sales Ledger.

Customer Receipts including Cash Sales are entered and allocated as follows:

 2 Sales

 5 Receipts

 1 Enter/Allocate Sales Ledger Receipts

The program will then display the Enter/Allocate Sales Ledger Receipts screen. This screen has three sections for the input of information, as follows:

Bank and Posing Details

Bank:	This is the bank account into which the receipt will be entered. In the case of Receipts, select 1 — Current Bank A/C, by 🔽 in the Bank field and selecting 1 — Current Bank A/C or simply press the number 1 for this account. In the case of credit notes, or the allocation of a receipt which has been entered but has not been allocated, there will be no bank account involved so accept 0 – None [Existing Receipt] by pressing the Tab key to move directly to Code.
Date:	The Sales Ledger date will be displayed. Press the Tab key to accept this date for receipts.

Code:	Enter the code for this customer. (Click the Code field name or press the F2 function key to display a list of customers.) In the case of a credit note or an unallocated receipt, the remaining details will be entered automatically. A list of all unallocated receipts and credit notes will be displayed.
Owed:	The outstanding balance for this customer will be displayed automatically.

Receipt Details

Slip Ref:	Enter the lodgement slip number for receipts.
Reconciled:	Indicates whether the lodgement is reconciled or not.
Cheque No:	Enter the number of the cheque received for receipts or the word Cash for cash sales. (Remember that cash sales must be entered here immediately after producing the invoice as the money is received immediately.)
Cheque Date:	Enter the lodgement date for receipts.
Descriptions:	Enter the word 'cash' when entering and allocating cash sales. SL Receipt will be displayed by pressing the Tab key. The Sales Credit Note will be displayed automatically when allocating credit notes.
Amount:	Enter the amount of the receipt. The amount of a credit note will be displayed automatically.
Unalloc:	The amount still unallocated will be displayed. If the receipt is being allocated against a number of invoices, then this amount will decrease as allocations are made. The allocation is complete when this figure is zero.

Cash/Credit for Allocation

Post No:	The posting number of the payment or credit note is displayed.
Type:	The journal type is displayed.
Inv/Rcpt No:	The invoice, credit note number is displayed.
Inv/Rcpt Date:	The invoice, cheque or credit note date is displayed.
Description:	The description of the posting is displayed.
Amount:	The amount of receipt or credit note is displayed.
Rem Bal/Unall:	The amount still due or unallocated is displayed.
S:	Indicates the status of the posting. The letter A indicates allocated.

When you have entered the data the screen will look like the following:

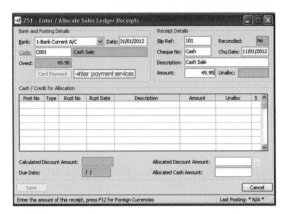

When you press the Tab key again, the following message will be displayed: When you have checked that all the information is correct, 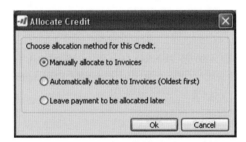 Yes and the following message will be displayed:

Manually allocate to Invoices should be selected automatically, provided this option was selected when setting the TASBooks configuration in page 84. OK and the Cash/Credit for Allocation section of the screen will change to Unpaid Invoices/Debits and display a list of the outstanding invoices for this customer.

If there were more than one invoice, then the mouse or the arrow keys would be used to select the invoice to which the payment/credit note relates.

Press the Tab key and the Allocate Discount Amount field will display 0.00. If there is a discount on this invoice it will be entered here.

Press the Tab key twice more to skip the Split Allocation ( ) and the Allocate Cash Amount field will display the amount to be allocated.

Press the Tab key once more to accept the amount of the allocation or enter the amount to be allocated and then press the Tab key. If the receipt/credit note is not for the full amount of the invoice then a window will appear on screen, informing you that this invoice is only part-paid.

A message asking you to confirm saving this receipt allocation will appear. Yes and the allocation is complete.

Enter and Allocate Customer Receipt

Monies are usually received from customers in the form of a cheque, and cheque payments must be entered and allocated in exactly the same way as a receipt of cash for a Cash Sale.

TASK C-8

Enter and Allocate the cheque received from James Mahon on Source Documents page 9.

The procedure for performing this task is the same as entering and allocating the receipt of the cash for the Cash Sale. The procedure is as follows:

 2 Sales

 5 Receipts

 1 Enter/Allocate Sales Ledger Receipts

The program will then display the Enter/Allocate Sales Ledger Receipts screen, as shown above.

In this case, the cheque number is entered instead of the word 'cash', and SL Receipt will appear automatically in the Description field when the tab key is pressed, instead of typing a description.

TASK C-9

Enter and Allocate the cheques received on Source Documents pages 9–10.

Allocate Customer (Sales) Credit Note

TASK C-10

Allocate the Credit Note on Source Documents page 2 issued to New Age Contractors.

When a credit note has been created and posted in the Sales Order section, it must also be allocated against the relevant invoice in the Sales section. For this purpose the credit note is treated as a part payment against the invoice, and therefore it must be allocated in the same way as a receipt in the Sales Ledger as follows:

 2 Sales

 5 Receipts

 1 Enter/Allocate Sales Ledger Receipts

The program will then display the Enter/Allocate Sales Ledger Receipts screen as shown above.

Credit notes have no connection with the Bank Current A/C, so the option 0 – None Existing Receipt is accepted by pressing the tab key. The cursor will move to the Code field. Click the Code field name or press the F2 function key to display a list of customers.

Select New Age Contractors and press the Tab key. The credit note will appear in the Cash/Credit for Allocation section of the screen. Press the Tab key and the following message will be displayed:

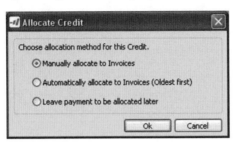

 OK and the Cash/Credit for Allocation section of the screen will change to Unpaid Invoices/Debits and display a list of the outstanding invoices for this customer.

Select the invoice and allocate as described above for receipt allocations.

Customer Account Enquiry

TASK C-11 (OPTIONAL)

Produce a report showing all the transactions for New Age Contractors.

This option is used to view the transactions contained in one particular customers account. The option is selected as follows:

 **2 Sales**

 **1 Customers**

 **2 Customer Account Enquiry**

The program then displays the screen used to enter new customers. (We will be entering new customers later.)

Click the Customer Code field name or press the F2 function key to display a list of customers. Select New Age Contractors and then press the Tab key. The details for that customer will then appear.

The program automatically defaults to displaying the Open (Unpaid) Items only (i.e. items that have not been cleared by being allocated or having a receipt and/or a credit note allocated against them for the full amount). If you wish to display all items, then the field at the bottom of the screen must be changed to display All Items. This is accomplished by  beside the window, displaying Open (Unpaid) Items. A short drop-down menu will appear, so simply click on All Items.

The screen should then look like the following:

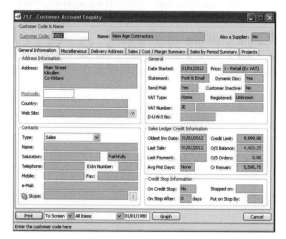

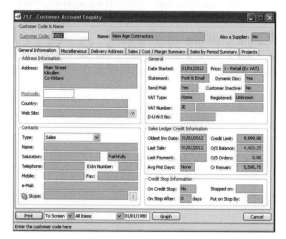 **Print** and the report will be displayed on the screen.

A hard copy of the report may be printed by simply 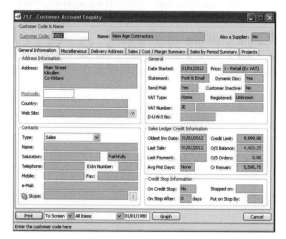 **Print Icon** 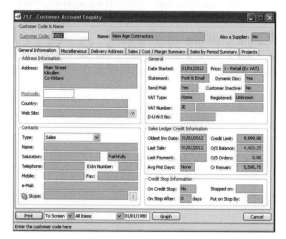 in the top left-hand corner of the screen display.

4 Purchase Ledger

The Purchase Ledger is used to store all the information relating to suppliers. All invoices, credit notes and payments are recorded in the Purchase Ledger. This includes invoices (bills) for telephone and electricity. When an invoice or credit notes is received it must firstly be entered into the Purchase Ledger.

Purchase Invoices

Every time a credit purchase is made, an invoice will be received by our company from the supplier. The data contained on this invoice must be entered into the computer accounts.

> **TASK C-12**
>
> Enter the details contained on the Purchase Invoice on Source Documents page 11 into the Purchase Ledger.

The procedure for entering purchase invoices into the Purchase Ledger is as follows:

3   **Purchase**

2   **Enter/Change Journals**

1   **Enter/Change Supplier Invoices/Credit Journals**

The program will then display the Enter/Change Supplier Invoices/Credit Journals screen.

There are three distinct sections to this screen for the input of information. The program will prompt you at the bottom of the screen with instructions. Remember to use the Tab key to move to the next field.

The required information is as follows:

Posting Details	
Department:	Enter the department number. It will always be 100 in the case of single-department businesses, in which case 100 will be displayed automatically.
Posting No:	This is a unique posting number issued by the program to each individual entry. Therefore it is left blank by the operator when inputting an invoice or credit note. Any entry may be altered by recalling this posting number. (The posting number for invoices or credit notes already entered may be obtained from the Purchase/Cash Daybooks. The procedure for obtaining this report is described later.)
Date:	The Purchase Ledger date will be displayed here. (This should be the last day of the current month. Do not change this date unless you are making a posting into a different month.)
Source:	Enter the source for this entry. The letters PL are displayed, indicating the Purchase Ledger.
Type:	Enter the type of entry. Accept PL Invoice.
Tip:	You may skip through this section by pressing the Tab key twice.
Invoice Details	
Code:	Enter the code for this supplier (creditor) and then press the Tab key. (Click the Code field name or press the F2 function key to display a list of suppliers.)
Name:	The name of the supplier will be displayed automatically once the code is entered.
Ref No:	Enter the invoice number as displayed on the invoice.
Date:	Enter the invoice date as displayed on the invoice.
Exp Pay Date:	Press the Tab key to accept the date offered.
Desc:	This is the description for this entry and Purchase Invoice will be displayed automatically once you press the Tab key.
Net:	This is the net amount as indicated on the invoice.
VAT:	This is the VAT code, followed by the amount as indicated on the invoice. The VAT amount will be calculated automatically, except in the case of Multi VAT (M) code (see below). (Pressing the F2 key will display the list of VAT codes.)
Total:	This is the total of Net plus VAT, and will be calculated automatically.
Rem Bal:	This is the amount of the outstanding balance on this invoice, and it will be equal to the total.
Disc:	This is the amount of discount on this entry. We will leave it blank by pressing the Tab key.

Nominal Ledger Details

The bottom half of the screen is for the Nominal Ledger distribution. This is where we perform the nominal ledger double entry for this transaction. The total of the Debit column must equal the total of the Credit column for a valid entry. If the totals are not equal then the program will indicate this.

Line 1 will be the Creditors account and will be a credit for the total of the invoice.

Line 2 will be the VAT Payable account and will debit the VAT amount.

The next line will allow you to debit the Expense or Asset account by the value of the goods on the invoice. If you have made an entry for this supplier, then the account will automatically appear and you will simply have to enter the correct amount in the Debit column. Otherwise, you will have to enter the correct Nominal Account Number under Account for the Purchase Account, and then enter the correct value. (Pressing the F2 function key will display a list of Nominal accounts.)

When you have entered the required details the screen should look like the following:

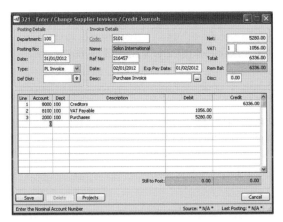

 Save and then **Yes** and the invoice will be saved.

TASK C-13

Enter the details contained on the Purchase Invoices on Source Documents pages 12–13 into the Purchase Ledger.

Enter and Allocate Purchase Credit Notes

TASK C-14

Enter the details contained on the Purchase Credit Note on Source Documents page 14 into the Purchase Ledger.

Credit notes that are received from suppliers must also be entered into the Purchase Ledger and allocated against the relevant invoice. Purchase credit notes are entered in the Purchase Ledger as follows:

3   **Purchase Ledger**

2   **Enter/Change Journals**

2   **Enter/Change Supplier Credit Notes/Debit Journals**

The screen display is the same as the Purchase Invoice screen. The entries made in the various sections are exactly the same as for the Purchase Invoice. VAT distribution should be input as with the invoice. In the case of a Purchase Credit Note, the Creditors account is debited by the amount of the credit note and the VAT Payable and Purchase accounts are credited with the respective amounts.

Note:

Remember that once you enter the credit note you must allocate it, that is to say, you must match the credit note to the relevant invoice in order to reduce the invoice by the amount of the credit note. The credit note is treated as a part payment against the invoice, and therefore it must be entered as a Payment into the Purchase Ledger.

When a credit note has been entered it must also be allocated against the relevant invoice. For this purpose the credit note is treated as a part payment against the invoice, and therefore it must be allocated in the same way as a Payment in the Purchase Ledger.

TASK C-15

Allocate the Credit Note on Source Documents page 14 received from Solon International.

Supplier Payments and Purchase Credit Notes are allocated as follows:

3 **Purchase**

5 **Payments on Account**

1 **Enter/Allocate Purchase Ledger Payments**

The program will then display the Enter/Allocate Purchase Ledger Payments screen.

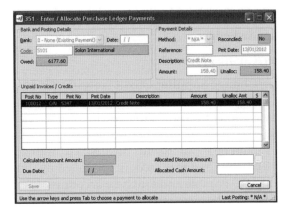

This screen has three sections for the input of information, as follows:

Bank and Posting Details	
Bank:	This is the bank account into which the payment will be entered. In the case of Payments select 1 – Current Bank A/C, by [ ] [ ] in the Bank field and selecting 1 – Current Bank A/C or simply press the number 1 for this account. In the case of a credit note or the allocation of a payment which has not been allocated, there will be no bank account involved, so accept 0 – None [Existing Payment] by pressing the Tab key to move directly to Code.
Date:	The Purchase Ledger date will be displayed. Press the Tab key to accept for payments.
Code:	Enter the code for this Supplier. (Click the Code field name or press the F2 function key to display a list of suppliers.) In the case of a credit note or an unallocated payment the remaining details will be entered automatically. A list of all unallocated payments and credit notes will be displayed
Owed:	The outstanding balance for this Supplier will be displayed automatically.
Payment Details	
Method	Select payment method; it is usually by cheque.
Reconciled:	Indicates whether a payment is reconciled or not.
Reference:	Enter the cheque number for payments. The credit note number will appear when allocating credit notes.
Pmt Date:	Enter the date on the cheque or remittance advice in the case of payments. The credit note date will be displayed for allocating credit notes.

Descriptions:	PL Payment will be displayed by pressing the Tab key. Credit Note will be displayed for allocating credit notes.
Amount:	Enter the amount of the payment. In the case of a credit note allocation, the credit note amount will be displayed.
Unalloc:	This field indicates the amount still unallocated.

Unpaid Invoices/Credits

Post No:	The posting number of the payment or credit note.
Type:	The journal type.
Pmt No:	Invoice or credit note number.
Pmt Date:	Invoice, cheque or credit note date.
Description:	Description of the posting.
Amount:	Amount of payment or credit note.
Unalloc Amt:	The amount still due or unallocated.
S:	Indicates the status of the posting.

To allocate credit notes, select the credit note to be allocated and then press the Tab key.

The following message will be displayed:

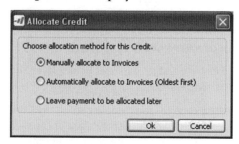

Manually allocate to Invoices should be selected, provided this option was selected when setting the TASBooks configuration in page 86. ▶ OK and the Cash/Credit for Allocation section of the screen will change to Unpaid Invoices/Credits and display a list of the outstanding invoices for this supplier. Select the correct invoice.

Press the Tab key and the Allocate Discount Amount field will display 0.00. If there is a discount on this invoice it will be entered here.

Press the Tab key twice more to skip the Split Allocation (▢) and the Allocate Cash Amount field will display the amount to be allocated.

Press the Tab key once more to accept the amount of the allocation or enter the amount to be allocated and then press the Tab key. If the payment or credit note is not for the full amount of the invoice, then a window will appear on screen informing you that this invoice is only part-paid. ▶ OK to continue the invoice amount will be reduced by the amount of the payment or credit note.

A message asking you to confirm saving this Payment allocation will appear. 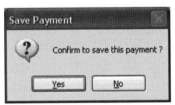 **Yes** and the allocation is complete.

Enter and Allocate Supplier Payments

Once a payment has been made to a Supplier (Creditor) it must be entered and allocated against the particular invoice to which it relates.

TASK C-16

Enter and Allocate the Remittance Advice for Philem Ireland on Source Documents page 15.

Payments to suppliers are usually accompanied with a remittance advice which details the payment being made. In our case, payments to suppliers are entered and allocated as follows:

3 Purchase

5 Payments on Account

1 Enter/Allocate Purchase Ledger Payments

The program will then display the Enter/Allocate Purchase Ledger Payments screen as shown above for allocating credit notes.

In this case the Bank Current A/C must be selected as the cheque is drawn on the bank. The details of the payment must be entered as described above.

When the payment details have been entered the following window will be displayed:

Save Payment

? Confirm to save this payment ?

Yes   No

Yes and then **OK** to the message to manually allocate to invoice.
Complete the allocation as described above for allocating a credit note.

TASK C-17

Enter and Allocate the Remittance Advice for Solon International on Source Documents page 16.

Purchase Daybooks

There are a great number of reports available from the computer program. The reports that are available for sales are also available for purchases. Some of these reports are very similar to the daybooks and ledgers as produced manually. There are also a number of extra reports that provide information not readily available from the manual system.

TASK C-18

Produce a purchase daybook report and compare this with your purchases/purchases returns daybook produced manually for January.

The purchase daybook is produced as follows:

 3 Purchase

 **4 Purchase Ledger Reports**   *or*

 1 Print Purchase/Cash Daybooks

When this option is selected the following screen will be displayed:

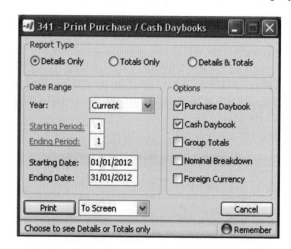

This report is actually two reports in one. It will produce a purchase daybook and a cash daybook. The cash daybook shown here is only a record of supplier payments and is not a cash (bank) payments report.

In this case the periods and dates for the report are correct. The tick for Cash Daybook should be removed in order to display the purchase daybook only.

 Print and the purchase daybook report will be displayed on screen. It may be a good idea to compare this report with the purchase/purchase returns daybook produced manually.

A hard copy of the report may be printed by simply **Print Icon** in the top left-hand corner of the screen display.

TASK C-19 (OPTIONAL)

Produce a report showing all the transactions for Solon International.

Supplier Account Enquiry

This option is used to view the transactions contained in one particular supplier's account. The option is selected as follows:

 3 Purchase

 1 Suppliers

 2 Supplier Account Enquiry

The program then displays the screen used to enter new Suppliers (we will be entering new suppliers later).

Click the Supplier Code field name or press the F2 function key to display a list of suppliers. Select Solon International and then press the tab key. The details for that supplier will then appear.

The program automatically defaults to displaying only the Open (Unpaid) Items (i.e. items that have not been cleared by being allocated or having a payment and/or a credit note allocated against them for the full amount). If you wish to display all items then the field at the bottom of the screen, must be changed to display All Items. This is accomplished by 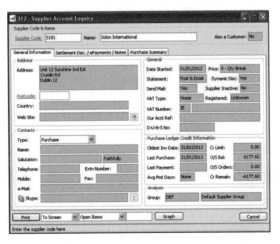 beside the window, displaying Open Items. A short drop-down menu will appear, so simply click on All Items.

The screen should then look like the following:

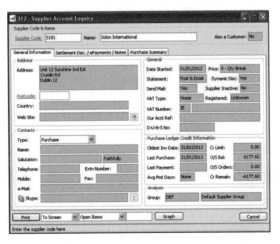

 Print and the report will be displayed on the screen.

A hard copy of the report may be printed by simply **Print Icon** 🖶 the top left-hand corner of the screen display.

5 Cash Book

The payment of salaries, rent, VAT, PAYE/PRSI, petty cash purchases, etc., are recorded in the Cash Book. The monies paid out are credited to the Bank Current A/C or the Petty Cash account. The purchase of some goods for which you do not wish to set up an account in the Purchase Ledger, but wish to pay for by cheque, may also be entered in the Cash Book, credited to the Bank Current A/C and debited to the correct Expense or asset account in the Nominal Ledger.

The computer version of Cash Book contains the equivalent of the Cash Receipts (Bank Lodgement) Book and the Cash (Bank) Payments Book on the manual system. The one exception is that the receipts from customers and the payments to suppliers are recorded in the respective ledgers. The program updates the Cash Book automatically with the details of the receipt or payment.

Payments from Bank Current Account

The entry of purchases that are not recorded in the purchase ledger and the payment of non-purchase payments such as salaries, rent, VAT, etc., are recorded in the cash book.

TASK C-20

A direct debit of €325.00 was made for rent on 30/01/##. Enter this payment into the cash book.

This payment is entered as follows:

▸ 4 Cash Book

▸ 2 Enter/Change Journals

▸ 2 Enter/Change Cash Payments/Purchases

The program then presents the Enter/Change Cash Payments/Purchases screen. This screen has three sections for the input of data, as follows:

Bank Account and Posting Details

Bank No:	This will be the Bank Account number. Select 1 – Bank Current A/C for cheque, Direct Debit or Standing Order payments. Select 2 – Petty Cash for petty cash purchases.
Posting No:	This is a unique posting number issued by the program to each individual entry. (Leave this blank unless recalling a posting). Any entry may be altered by recalling this posting number. (The posting number for invoices or credit notes already entered may be obtained from the Cash Book Payments/Receipts report. The procedure for obtaining this report is described later).
Date:	Enter the date for this transaction.
Type:	Home Purchase will be displayed but you may select from list by ⬆ ▾ and selecting from the list. In the case of rent, salaries, etc., that have no VAT associated with them, select Non-VAT Jnl.
Chq/Ref:	This will be the cheque number, the DD or SO in the case of Current A/C payments, or the voucher number in the case of petty cash payments.
Desc:	Type a description for this payment, e.g. Salaries, Rent Payment etc. In the case of petty cash enter the item(s) purchased.

Amounts

Net Amt:	This is the net amount of this payment.
VAT Amt:	This is the VAT code, followed by the amount of VAT on the payment. The VAT amount will be calculated automatically, except in the case of the Multi-VAT (M) code. (Pressing the F2 key will display the list of VAT codes).
Total Amt:	This is the total of Net plus VAT and will be calculated automatically.

Nominal Ledger Details

The bottom half of the screen is for the Nominal Ledger distribution. This is where we perform the nominal ledger double entry for this transaction. The total of the Debit column must equal the total of the Credit column for a valid entry. If the totals are not equal then the program will indicate this.

Line 1 will be the Bank Current A/C and will be a credit for the total of the payment.

Line 2 will be the VAT payable account, if there is VAT on the payment, and will debit the VAT amount.

The next line will allow you to debit the Expense or Asset account(s) with the value of the payment. Enter the correct Nominal Account Number, under Account for the account to be debited and then enter the correct value in the debit column. (Pressing the F2 function key will display a list of nominal accounts).

When you have entered all the details the screen should look like the following:

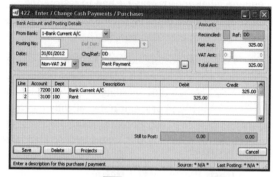

Once the double entry is correct ▸ **Save** and then ▸ **Yes** to confirm to save the transaction.

Petty Cash Purchases

Small items that are purchased from time to time are not normally entered in the Purchase Ledger and paid for by cheque. Instead, a certain amount of cash is withdrawn from the Bank Current A/C at regular intervals and kept as petty cash in order to purchase small items. Each time a purchase is made using this cash, a voucher is completed, and in some cases must be authorised. The entry of these purchases is recorded in a special bank account, called 'Petty Cash' in the Cash Book.

TASK C-21

Enter the petty cash vouchers on Source Documents pages 17–19 into the Cash Book.

This payment is entered as follows:

▸ **4 Cash Book**

▸ **2 Enter/Change Journals**

▸ **2 Enter/Change Cash Payments/Purchases**

The entry of petty cash vouchers is the same as for payments from the current bank account, as described above.

Restore Petty Cash Imprest

The first task to be performed at the end of each month (or some other regular interval) is to calculate the amount spent from petty cash and to restore the imprest to the correct amount. The company decides how much money should be in petty cash at the start of each month. This amount is called the 'imprest', and it must be restored at the end of each month before moving on to the next month's transactions.

TASK C-22

On the 31/01/## cheque number 200103 was cashed to restore the petty cash imprest. Calculate the amount of this cheque and enter it into Cash Book.

This payment is very similar to any Cash Book Payment, but since the money is being paid into another one of our bank accounts (petty cash) there is a slight difference, so this entry is explained separately. Restoring the petty cash imprest is accomplished as follows:

▶ **4 Cash Book**

▶ **2 Enter/Change Journals**

▶ **2 Enter/Change Cash Payments/Purchases**

The program then presents the Enter/Change Cash Payments/Purchases screen, as explained above.

In the first section of this screen, instead of accepting Home Purch, ▶ ▼ in the Type field and select Inter-Bank. Once you enter the net amount, the program will display the following screen:

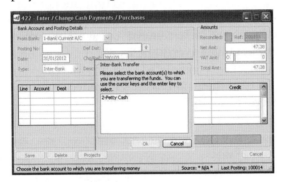

 2 – Petty Cash and then ▶ **OK**.

The program will then complete the double entry, so just ▶ **Yes** to save the transaction.

Cash Receipts (including Start-up Capital Investment)

Any monies received by the company that are not from customers must also be lodged to the bank and recorded in the company books. When a company sets up business and prepares to start trading, it invariably needs capital. This capital investment must be recorded in the company accounts and is usually the first entry in the books.

In the manual system, this entry of capital investment was recorded in the General Journal. In the computerised bookkeeping system, this entry may also be recorded in the general journal, but it is more common and correct to record the entry in the Cash Book. The entry will include the nominal accounts used in the entry and the program will automatically update the Nominal Ledger.

TASK C-23

J.P. Murphy commenced business on 01/01/## with a capital investment of €15,000.00. €14,900.00 of this was deposited in their current bank account and €100.00 was placed in petty cash. Use the General Journal to record these entries.

Cash received that is not received as a result of issuing a Sales Invoice is normally entered into the Cash Book. The entry of Capital Investment is normally recorded as a cash receipt in the Bank Current A/C. If the petty cash imprest is retained, then it is also recorded as a cash receipt into the petty cash account.

The procedure for entering Cash Receipts into the Cash Book is as follows:

4 Cash Book

2 Enter/Change Journals

1 Enter/Change Cash Receipts/Sales

The program then presents the Enter/Change Cash Receipts/Sales screen which is very similar to the cash payments screen. This screen has three sections for the input of data as follows:

Bank Account and Posting Details

Bank No:	This will be the Bank Account number. Select 1 – Bank Current A/C for the money lodged to the bank. Select 2 – Petty Cash for the petty cash amount.
Posting No:	This is a unique posting number issued by the program to each individual entry. Any entry may be altered by recalling this posting number.
Date:	Enter the date for this transaction.
Type:	Home Receipt will be displayed but you may select from list by [S] and selecting from the list. In the case Capital investment, which have no VAT associated with it, select Non-VAT Jnl.
Slip No:	This will be the Lodgement Slip Number. Enter 100 for the lodgement of the capital to the Bank Current A/C. Leave blank for the Petty Cash entry.
Desc:	Type a description for this receipt, e.g. Start-up Capital Investment in this case.

Amounts

Net Amt: This is the net amount of this receipt.

VAT Amt: This is the VAT code, followed by the amount of VAT on the payment.
                Enter 9 for the Outside Scope Rate as there is no VAT attached to
                this transaction.

Total Amt: This is the total of Net plus VAT and will be calculated automatically.

Nominal Ledger Details

The bottom half of the screen is for the Nominal Ledger distribution. This is where we
perform the Nominal Ledger double entry for this transaction. The total of the Debit
column must equal the total of the Credit column for a valid entry. The program will
indicate if the totals are not equal.

    Line 1 will be the bank account (either current a/c or petty cash) and will be a
Debit for the total of the receipt.

    Line 2 will allow you to credit the Income or Owner Equity account(s) with the net
value of this receipt. Enter the correct Nominal Account Number under Account for the
account to be credited and then enter the correct value in the credit column.

    (In this case 9000 for the Capital account)

Once the data has been entered the screen should look like the following:

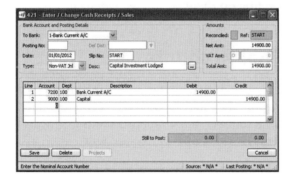

 Save and then **Yes** to confirm to save the transaction.

It is now necessary to enter the receipt for €100.00 into the Petty Cash
account. The process is exactly the same as the above, except this time, select
2 – Petty Cash as the Bank No. The details for the entry will be the same,
except that the amount will be €100.00.

6 Nominal Ledger

The Nominal (General) Ledger consists of a number of accounts that are used to record the Income, Expenditure, Assets, Liabilities and Owner Equity in the company. Every transaction that occurs in the company must be recorded eventually in the Nominal Ledger. Figures are transferred from the Sales Ledger, Purchase Ledgers and cash book automatically. The figures in the Nominal accounts are used in producing a trial balance.

Nominal accounts will be one of five possible types: Income, Expense, Asset, Liability or Owner Equity, as described on page 42 for manual bookkeeping. Each type of account will be either a Debit (Dr) or Credit (Cr) account. A Credit account will normally have a balance that is a Credit amount, and a Debit account will normally have a balance that is a Debit amount. The computer will automatically assign an account as 'Debit A/C' or 'Credit A/C' depending on the type entered when creating the account.

Enter/Create Nominal Accounts

The Nominal accounts required by the company must be created in the Nominal Ledger before they may be used when entering data. You have already been using a number of Nominal accounts as at least two must be used in order to make a valid entry in the accounts.

TASK C-24

Enter (Create) the following Nominal accounts:

Number	Description	Type	Group	Dr or Cr
3000	Salaries	Expense	Expense	Dr
3200	Electricity	Expense	Expense	Dr

New Nominal accounts are created as follows:

1 Nominal

1 Nominal Accounts

1 Maintain Chart of Accounts

The program will then present the Maintain Chart of Accounts screen.

The creation of a new account only requires the input the following information for each Nominal account:

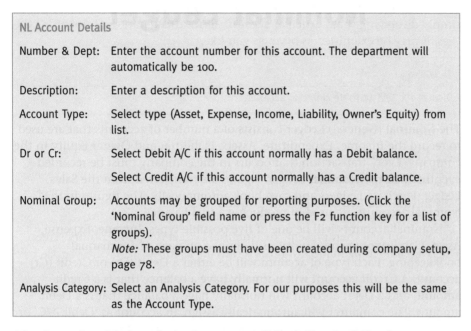

NL Account Details

Number & Dept: Enter the account number for this account. The department will automatically be 100.

Description: Enter a description for this account.

Account Type: Select type (Asset, Expense, Income, Liability, Owner's Equity) from list.

Dr or Cr: Select Debit A/C if this account normally has a Debit balance.

Select Credit A/C if this account normally has a Credit balance.

Nominal Group: Accounts may be grouped for reporting purposes. (Click the 'Nominal Group' field name or press the F2 function key for a list of groups).
Note: These groups must have been created during company setup, page 78.

Analysis Category: Select an Analysis Category. For our purposes this will be the same as the Account Type.

After inputting the data above the screen will look like the following:

 **Save** and then  **Yes** to save this account.

Nominal Ledger Account Enquiry

All transactions entered in the company books must appear in one of the Nominal accounts. Any Nominal account may be examined at any time by simply displaying that particular account. Since this report does not affect the files, it may be examined as often as you like.

TASK C-25

Display the VAT Payable Nominal account.

A Nominal account is displayed as follows:

1 Nominal

1 Nominal Accounts

2 Nominal Ledger Account Enquiry

The program will then present the Nominal Ledger Account Enquiry screen. The selections to be made from this screen are as follows:

Account	
Number & Dept:	Click the Number & Dept field name or press the F2 and select the Nominal account number.
Department:	100 will be displayed automatically.
Date Range	
Year:	The current year will be displayed, but you may select past years for which details are required.
Starting Period:	Period 1 will be displayed, but you may enter any starting period. *Note:* The first period is the first month of the financial year, not necessarily January.
Ending Period:	Period 1 will be displayed because we are still dealing with month 1. The program will automatically display the number of the period with which you are currently working.
The Starting and Ending dates will be displayed automatically when the periods are entered.	
Options	
Include Opening Balance: Tick this box to display the opening balance for this account.	

When the data has been entered the screen will look like the following:

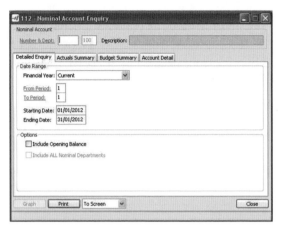

 **Print** and the account details will be displayed on screen.

A hard copy of the report may be printed by simply  **Print Icon** ⬛ in the top left-hand corner of the screen display.

Print Trial Balance

Because all entries in the accounts are posted automatically to the Nominal Ledger, it is possible to produce a trial balance at any time. The computer simply prints the balances from each Nominal account. Since all entries in the system were balanced as they were entered, the trial balance will always balance. This does not mean that all the entries in the system were correct; the trial balance should be examined closely to make sure that it is correct.

TASK C-26

Display a trial balance as at 31/01/##.

The term 'as at' is used in accounting to mean from the start of the financial year up to the date stated.

A trial balance is produced as follows:

1 Nominal

3 Reporting

4 Print Trial Balance

The program will then present the Print Trial Balance screen. The selections to be made from this screen are as follows:

Date Range

Year:　　　　　　　The current year will be displayed, but you may select past years for which a trial balance is required.

Starting Period:　Period 1 and the date will be displayed, but you may enter any starting period.

Ending Period:　　Period 1 will be displayed because we are still dealing with month 1. The program will automatically display the number of the period with which you are currently working.

Options

Include:　　　　　Tick the box for Year-to-date Figures.

When the data has been entered the screen will look like the following:

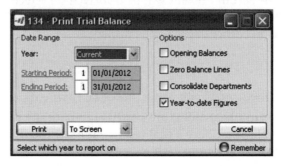

Print and the trial balance will be displayed on screen. The report may be sent to the printer in the normal way.

Note:

Compare this trial balance with the one produced manually for the same period. Both trial balances should be exactly the same.

7 Customers and Suppliers

A company will normally have a number of customers and suppliers. All information about customers, including transactions, is stored in the Sales Ledger. All information about suppliers, including transactions, is stored in the Purchase Ledger.

Set Up New Customer and Supplier

In order to enter Invoices, Credit Notes, Receipts, Payments, etc., the standing data, such as name, address and phone number must be set up for each customer or supplier.

TASK C-27

Set up the standing data for the customer and supplier listed below:

Customer

Code	D001
Name	Francis Dunne
Address	Cutlery Road
	Newbridge
	Co Kildare
Phone	045-433258
Fax	
e-mail	

Supplier

Code	P102
Name	Power Ireland
Address	Park West
	Navan
	Co Meath
Phone	046-253672
Fax	046-253489
e-mail	info@powerirl.ie

The procedure for setting up customers and suppliers is practically identical, so the following steps relate to both. Standing data is set up as follows:

Customers	Suppliers
▶ 2 Sales	▶ 3 Purchase
▶ 1 Customers	▶ 1 Suppliers
▶ 1 Maintain Customers	▶ 1 Maintain Suppliers

The program will then present a screen for the input of the standing data for each customer/supplier.

This screen contains five different sections: General Information, Miscellaneous, Delivery Address, NL Distribution and Documents. These are displayed as tabs under the customer/supplier code and name, and may be selected simply by clicking on the tab name. You may ignore much of the data in the various sections.

The data that you will need to enter is contained on the General Information section and is as follows:

Customer/ Supplier Code:	The code for this customer/supplier.
Name:	The name of this customer/supplier.
Also a Customer /Supplier:	If this customer is also a supplier, or vice versa, then select Yes. Alternately, accept No by pressing the Tab key.
Address:	The customer's/supplier's address.
Telephone:	Customer's/supplier's telephone number.
Fax:	Customer's/supplier's fax number.
e-Mail:	Customer's/supplier's e-mail address.
Credit Limit:	Enter 9999.00 – this will prevent a warning message from appearing when you enter Sales Orders.
Note:	Use the Tab key to move from field to field and to skip a field.

When you have entered the information above, the screen should look like the following for entering a customer:

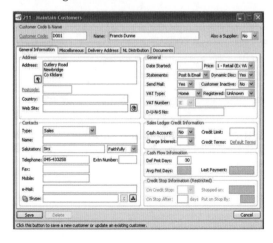

Save, to save and then **Yes** to confirm to save this customer/supplier.

Unallocate/Delete Receipt or Payment

Sometimes a receipt or payment may have been allocated incorrectly, or the payment may have been entered on the wrong customer's or supplier's account. If the receipt/payment has been allocated incorrectly, then it must be unallocated. If it was entered on the wrong account, then it must be deleted in order to be entered on and allocated to the correct account. During the unallocation procedure, you can decide whether to unallocate and retain the receipt/payment, or whether to delete it altogether.

TASK C-28 (OPTIONAL)

Unallocate and delete the receipt from The Electrical Shop.

Receipts/payments are unallocated as follows:

Customers	Suppliers
2 Sales	**3 Purchase**
5 Receipts	**5 Payments on Account**
2 Unallocate/Delete Sales Ledger Receipts	**2 Unallocate/Delete Purchase Ledger Payments**

The program will then display a screen for the input of some data, as follows:

Customer/Supplier Details

Code & Name: Enter the customer's/supplier's code and press the Tab key. The Name will be displayed automatically.
(Click the Code & Name field name or press the F2 function key to display a list of customers.)

Start Date: Enter a date to start the search for receipts or payments. In cases where there are large volumes of receipts/payments, entering a start date is a simple method of reducing the amount of receipts/payments to be displayed.

Display: You must click [Display] order to display the receipts/payments, or press the enter key when the display button is active (highlighted).

Note: Use the Tab key to move from field to field or to skip a field.

Enter the data and 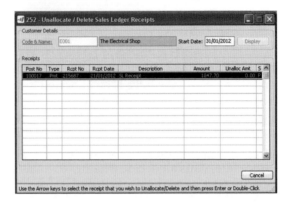 **Display,** and the following screen will be displayed:

If there is more than one payment, select the receipt/payment to be unallocated by using the arrow keys or the mouse, and press the enter key. The following screen will then be displayed:

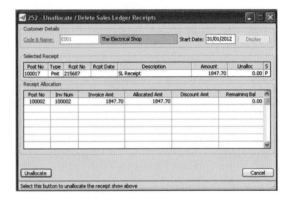

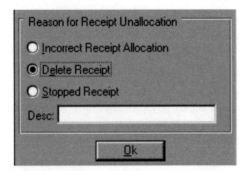 Unallocate and the following window will appear:

At this stage you may decide whether to unallocate or to delete the receipt/payment altogether.

Delete Receipt Point to Delete Receipt and click the left mouse button.

OK and the unallocation and deletion are complete.

TASK C-29 (OPTIONAL – BUT MUST BE PERFORMED IF TASK C-28 IS COMPLETED)

Enter and allocate the receipt on page 9 from The Electric Shop.

This will restore the company files to their original position before we deleted the receipt.

8 Products and Services

In order to produce an invoice using the invoicing section of a computerised bookkeeping program, it is necessary to have the details about the products and services that the company sells entered into the computer records. Each product is given a code that is then used to access that product for the purpose of issuing invoices and credit notes.

Enter Product Details

The computer program offers a special section for entering the details about products and services.

TASK C-30

Add the following product in the list of products:

Code	Description	VAT Rate	Retail Price
T122	22" Solon TV	1–21%	€299.00

The task of adding to the list of products and services is completed as follows:

▶ **5 Stock**

▶ **1 Products and Services**

▶ **1 Maintain Product / Service**

The program then presents a screen for the input of the required data for each product/service.

The top of this screen is headed Product Code and Description and requires the input of the following:

Product Code and Description	
Code:	Enter the code for this Product/Service.
Description:	Enter the description for this Product/Service.

The rest of the screen has five sections, with tabs labelled General Information, Nominal/Supplier/Intrastat, Assembly Details, Picture, and Documents. The General Information section requires the data for each product, and the Nominal section requires the selection of some Nominal accounts associated with the product/service. We will not be dealing with the other sections at this level. At the bottom of the screen, you will see a prompt for the data required in each field.

The data required is detailed below. Press the Tab key to skip the fields where you do not have to enter data. In some cases the program will enter default values, and in other cases the field will remain blank.

GENERAL INFORMATION

General

Product Type:	Select from one of three types:	Assembly
		Non-stock item (i.e. Service)
		Regular stock item

In our case we will be dealing with regular stock items, so press the Tab key to accept this option.

VAT Rate: Select the appropriate VAT rate for this Product/Service. (Click the down arrow icon to display the list of VAT codes).

Press the Tab key to accept the default values for the rest of the General section.

Retail Pricing

Retail: This is the price including VAT. The program will calculate this automatically when the price is entered in Retail (Ex. VAT).

Press the Tab key to skip this section.

Standard Pricing

Retail (Ex. VAT): Enter the normal selling price, excluding VAT.

Press the Tab key to skip the rest of this section.

Quantity Discounts

This section is used to enter discounts for quantity purchases. The price will automatically be entered in Sell Price 1.

Press the Tab key to skip this section and move onto the Nominal/Supplier/Intrastat section.

When you have entered the General Information the screen should look like the following:

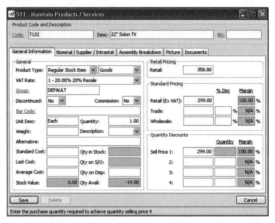

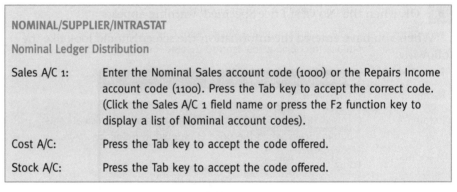

Nominal/Supplier/Intrastat tab and enter the following data. (Continue to press the Tab key in the general section and the Nominal/Supplier/Intrastat section will automatically be displayed.)

NOMINAL/SUPPLIER/INTRASTAT

Nominal Ledger Distribution

Sales A/C 1: Enter the Nominal Sales account code (1000) or the Repairs Income account code (1100). Press the Tab key to accept the correct code. (Click the Sales A/C 1 field name or press the F2 function key to display a list of Nominal account codes).

Cost A/C: Press the Tab key to accept the code offered.

Stock A/C: Press the Tab key to accept the code offered.

When you have entered the **Nominal Ledger Distribution** information the screen should look like the following:

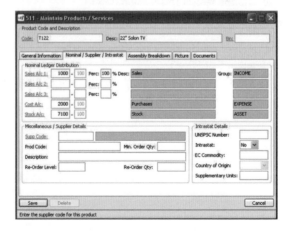

Save and then **Yes** to conform to save this product.

The program will then ask if you wish to enter an opening balance for this product.

 Yes and a screen will be displayed that allows you to enter an opening quantity.

(Entering an opening stock quantity now will prevent 'nil stock' error messages appearing when you produce sales orders.)

Enter the following information:

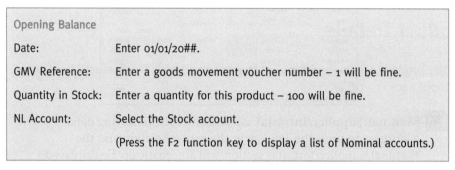

Opening Balance	
Date:	Enter 01/01/20##.
GMV Reference:	Enter a goods movement voucher number – 1 will be fine.
Quantity in Stock:	Enter a quantity for this product – 100 will be fine.
NL Account:	Select the Stock account.
	(Press the F2 function key to display a list of Nominal accounts.)

 OK when the 'No Cost Price Specified' warning appears.

When you have entered the information the screen should look like the following:

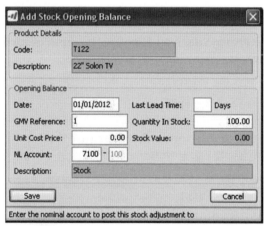

 Save and then **OK** and the product will be saved.

TASK C-31

Add the following products in the list of products:

Code	Description	VAT Rate	Retail Price
C101	CD Player (Philem)	1–21%	€85.00
V102	Panview DVD Player	1–21%	€249.00

Print Product Details

The product details report is used to print the details for products/services as input above.

TASK C-32

Print the Details of all products for J.P. Murphy Electric.

This option to print the products/services details is selected as follows:

5 Products

3 Products/Services Reporting

1 Print Product Details

The program then displays a screen allowing the input of some options as shown below:

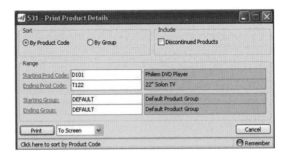

The options displayed are correct, so simply **Print** to display the report.
A hard copy of the report may be printed by simply **Print Icon** in the top left-hand corner of the screen display.

9 Report Printing

There are a great number of reports that may be obtained from the various ledgers. Running these reports causes the program to search the company files and assemble the required information in an understandable format. The running of any of these reports does not update the files; therefore they can be run as often as required.

The program defines how the reports are presented, so it is therefore only necessary to select the report required and input some simple selections for each report. Each report will provide prompts with the most likely options and, generally, it is only necessary to press the Tab key to accept the options offered. The prompt line at the bottom of the screen will provide instructions with what to input each time a piece of data is required.

Most reports require the input of the Starting and Ending Periods or the Starting and Ending Dates for the report. When inputting Starting and Ending periods (months) it must be remembered that Period 1 is the first period of the financial year for the company. This can be any month of the year, so it is not necessarily January. The period numbers are then counted from the first month of the financial year.

A hard copy of the report may be printed by simply ▶ **Print Icon** 🖨 in the top left-hand corner of the screen display. Click the Cancel button if you do not want to send it to the printer. This will close the window and return you to the previous window, where you may look at another report or ▶ **Cancel** to close the window.

The following reports have already been explained. The numbers in brackets indicate the menus selected to produce the report. The page number is the page number in this book where the report is explained.

Sales Order Enquiry	(6 3 1)	page 109
Sales Daybooks	(2 4 1)	page 112
Customer Account Enquiry	(2 1 2)	page 117
Purchase Daybooks	(3 4 1)	page 126
Supplier Account Enquiry	(3 1 2)	page 127
Nominal Ledger Account Enquiry	(1 1 2)	page 136
Print Trial Balance	(1 3 4)	page 137
Print Product Details	(5 3 1)	page 148

VAT Report

The VAT report provides the details required for filling in the VAT 3 form.

TASK C-33

Produce a VAT 100 report for January ##.

The VAT 100 report is produced as follows:

 0 Central

 3 VAT Rates/Reporting   *or*   VAT 3

 3 VAT Return Manager

When this option is selected, the program displays the following screen:

Ensure that the month and year are correct. (Since we have selected two monthly returns, we must select February.)

Note:

Ensure that the year is correct (the program will take the year from the computer clock, which may not be the year that you are using).

 Finish and the VAT 3 details will be displayed on screen.

It is a good idea to delete the report once it has been viewed, as you will not be returning this report to the Collector General. Deleting the report will allow you run it again without any difficulties.

Aged Debtors' Report

This is one of the most common reports to be produced on a computerised bookkeeping system. The report shows all the customers who owe money to the company.

TASK C-34

Produce an Aged Debtors' Report as at 31 January ##.

The Aged Debtors' Report is produced as follows:

 **2 Sales Ledger**

 **4 Sales Ledger Reports**

 **2 Print Aged Debtors' Report**

When this option is selected the program displays a screen for the input of some selections, as shown below:

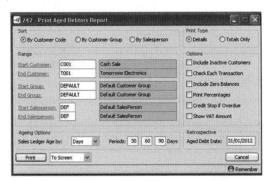

The options displayed on this screen are correct so  **Print** and the report will be displayed on screen showing details of all customers who owe money to the company.

Aged Creditors' Report

This shows all the suppliers to whom the company owes money:

TASK C-35

Produce an Aged Creditors' Report as at 31 January ##.

The Aged Creditors' Report is produced as follows:

 **3 Purchase Ledger**

 **4 Purchase Ledger Reports**

 **2 Print Aged Creditors' Report**

When this option is selected the program displays a screen for the input of some selections, as shown below:

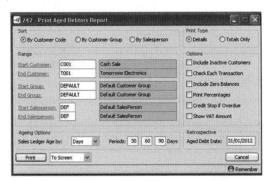

The options displayed on this screen are correct, so  **Print** and the report will be displayed on screen showing details of all suppliers who are owed money by the company.

Cash Book Payments and Receipts Reports

Cash Book Payments and Receipts Reports are displayed very often, as they provide a list of all monies paid out and received by the company. These reports should not be confused with the receipts and payments reports from the Sales and Purchases Ledger. These reports must be produced for each bank account separately, so it is necessary to produce separate reports for the Bank Current A/C and Petty Cash.

TASK C-36

Produce a Cash/Cheque Payments and Receipts report for January ##.

The task asks for a Cash/Cheque Payments and Receipts report, which indicates that you must create a report on the Bank Current A/C.

The Cash/Cheque Payments and Receipts report is produced as follows:

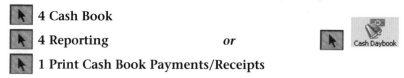

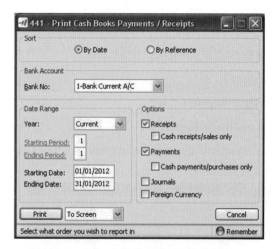

When this last option is selected, the program will display a screen requesting further information, as shown below:

In this case, the options offered are correct, as the options to print Cash Receipts and Cash Payments ticked, so  **Print** and the reports will be displayed on screen. If you only need one report, then simply remove the tick from the report that is not required.

The reports are displayed with one report in front of the other. The second report may be seen by moving or closing the first report to reveal the second one.

Petty Cash Payments Report

This report shows all the petty cash payments. Each item purchased from petty cash is listed on the report.

TASK C-37

Produce a Petty Cash Payments report for January ##.

The Petty Cash Payments report is produced using the same options as for the Cash/Cheques Payments and Receipts report as explained above. The report is displayed as follows:

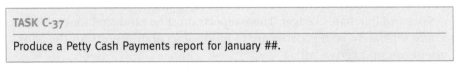 **4 Cash Book**

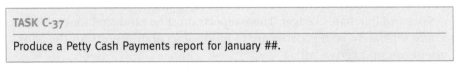 **4 Reporting**   *or*   Cash Daybook

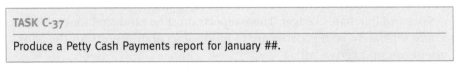 **1 Print Cash Book Payments / Receipts**

When this last option is selected, the program will display a screen requesting further information, as shown below. In this case you must select 2 – Petty Cash as the Bank Account No and remove the tick from Cash Receipts, as we only require the Petty Cash Payments report.

 Print and the report will be displayed on screen showing details of all petty cash payments for the month of January ##.

Note:

Any report displayed on screen may be sent to the printer by simply Print Icon 🖨 in the top left-hand corner of the screen display.

10 Bank Reconciliation

A bank reconciliation is a process used to explain the difference between the balance in the bank statement received from the company's bank and the corresponding balance shown in the company's own bank account record. There will usually be differences between the two bank statements.

The differences are usually due to one or more of the following reasons:

- A lodgement made by the company does not appear on the bank statement from the bank.
- A cheque issued by the company has not been presented to the bank and therefore does not appear on the bank statement from the bank.
- An error made by the bank.
- An error made by the company in its own bank account records.

The bank reconciliation process is used to identify the differences in the balances and make adjustments in order to equalise the balance figures. A completed bank reconciliation will result in both the adjusted bank balance (as per the bank statement) and the adjusted balance in the company's bank record (the bank account in the Nominal (General) Ledger) being equal.

TASK C-38

Perform a bank reconciliation using the bank statement on Source Documents, page 20 and the bank account in the Nominal (General) Ledger.

The first step in completing a bank reconciliation is to compare the bank statement with the Cash Receipts Book and the Cash Payments Book and identify any differences between them.

A bank reconciliation is performed by completing two calculations. The first calculation makes adjustments to the bank statement as follows:

Balance as per bank statement	€16,750.05
Adjustments:	
Add deposits not shown on bank statement	+ €0.00
Subtract cheques issued but not shown on bank statement	− €47.38
Subtract any payments recorded in own accounts but not shown on bank statement (e.g. DD or SO)	− €0.00
Adjusted Bank Balance	€16,702.67

The second calculation makes adjustments to the bank account in the Nominal (General) Ledger as follows:

Balance as per bank Nominal Ledger	€16,728.52
Adjustments:	
Add Interest earned	+ €0.00
Subtract bank charges	− €25.85
Add/Subtract any errors in Nominal bank account	+ €0.00
Adjusted Bank Nominal Ledger	€16,702.67

The Bank Reconciliation is complete when the two balance figures are the same.

11 Ledger Dates

When you start TASBooks Accounting Plus and enter the accounts for a particular company, there will be four dates displayed at the bottom of the screen, as shown below:

NL: 31/01/2012   SL: 31/01/2012   PL: 31/01/2012   09/12/2011

The four dates are the posting dates for the three ledgers and the present date. Some companies have all four dates set to the present date, and therefore, the dates will change automatically each day as the program takes the data from the computer clock when it starts up.

However, in some cases, such as at an accountant's office, work is done on a monthly basis. Therefore the ledger dates, i.e. Nominal Ledger (NL), Sales Ledger (SL) and Purchase Ledger (PL) are set to the end of the month. In our case, since we will not be working with an actual company, the dates we will be using will not be the present dates; we will use the end-of-month dates, and therefore, we will have to set the ledger dates at the start of each month before entering any transactions for that month.

Setting the Ledger Date

The ledger date may be set at any time, but is normally set at the start of each month.

TASK C-38

Set the Nominal Ledger date to the last day of February ##.

The ledger date is set as follows:

2 Sales

9 End of Period Programs *or*   NL: 31/01/2012

9 Change Sales Ledge Date

The program will display the Change Nominal Ledger Date window.

Enter the date required, i.e. the last day of the month.

Set the Set to today's date at start up option to '**No**'.

 Save to save new date.

TASK C-39

Set the Sales Ledger and Purchase Ledger dates to the last day of February ##.

12 Back Up and Restore Company Data Files

It is frequently necessary to copy the data files to back up storage (hard disc, CD, DVD or memory stick) and copy them from the backup storage back into the working folder when they are required again. In order to perform these operations, the company must be closed down within the program.

The TASBooks program provides an option for this purpose on the TASBooks Company Manager window. This window appears automatically when the program is started, or it may be selected from the Taskbar by simply pointing to it on the taskbar and clicking the left mouse button.

Note:

The company must *not* be open when backing up the data files.

TASK C-40

Backup the data files for J.P. Murphy Electric to back up storage.

Backing Up

1 Open the TASBooks Company Manager window. The window will appear as shown:

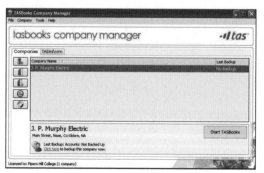

2 **Company name** (J.P. Murphy Electric will already be selected
if that is the only company setup on the computer)

3 **Back up icon** 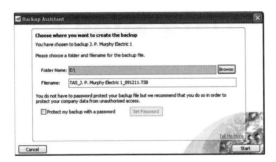 on the left-hand side or the Click here link at
the bottom of the window.
The program will then display the following window:

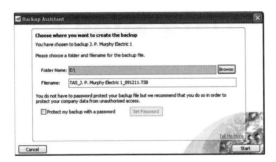

Select the folder or memory stick for the back-up files.

4 **Start** The back up will start and a progress window will be displayed
while the operation is taking place.
When backup is complete the following window will be displayed:

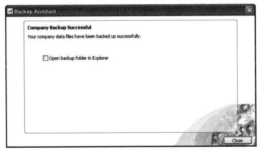

5 **Close** and the TASBooks Company Manager window will be
displayed again.

TASK C-41

Restore the data files for J.P. Murphy Electric from the backup storage.

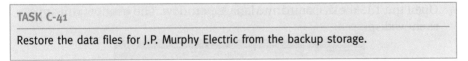

Restore

1   Open the TASBooks Company Manager window. The window will appear as shown:

2    **Company name** (J.P. Murphy Electric will already be selected if that is the only company setup on the computer.)

3   **Restore icon** on the left-hand side.

The program will then display the following window:

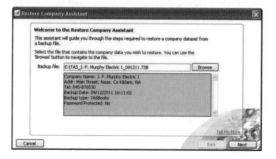

4   Highlight the file displayed and **Open.** The following window will then be displayed:

5  **Next** and the following window will be displayed:

6 Tick the box and 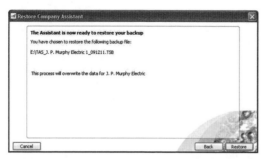 **Next**.

7 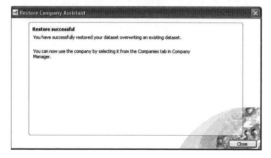 **Restore** Restoration will start and a progress window will be displayed while the operation is taking place.

When restoration is complete the following window will be displayed:

The program will then display the following window:

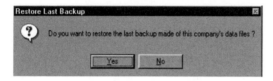

8  Yes and the following window will be displayed:

The data displayed is correct.

9 Restore and the program will restore the files to the hard disk, and will briefly display a progress window as it does so. When the restoration is complete, the following window will be displayed:

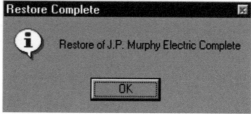

10 OK and the TASBooks Accounting Plus Multi Company Selection window will be displayed.

13 **Transaction Summary**

Source Documents

Sales Invoice

Sales Credit Note

Debtor Receipt

Enter Payment in Sales Ledger   page 116
    2 Sales
        5 Receipts
            1 Enter/Allocate Sales Ledger Receipts

Purchase Invoice

Enter Invoice in Purchase section   page 119
    3 Purchase
        2 Enter/Change Journals
            1 Enter/Change Supplier Invoices/Credit Journals

Purchase Credit Note

(a)   Enter Credit Note in Purchase section   page 121
    3 Purchase
        2 Enter/Change Journals
            2 Enter/Change Supplier Credit Note/Debit Journals

(b)   Allocate Credit Note in Purchase Ledger   page 122
    3 Purchase
        5 Payments on Account
            1 Enter/Allocate Purchase Ledger Payments

Creditor Payment (Remittance Advice)

Enter Payment in Purchase section   page 125
    3 Purchase
        5 Payments on Account
            1 Enter/Allocate Purchase Ledger Payments

Petty Cash Purchase

Enter Purchase in Cash Book   page 130
    4 Cash Book
        2 Enter/Change Journals
            2 Enter/Change Cash Payments/Purchases
            (Use 2 – Petty Cash as Bank account)

Non-Purchase Payment (Salaries, Rent, etc.)

Enter Payment in Cash Book   page 128
    4 Cash Book
        2 Enter/Change Journals
            2 Enter/Change Cash Payments/Purchases
            (Use **1** – Current Bank A/C)

Restore Petty Cash Imprest

Calculate the amount to be transferred by printing the petty cash daybook
and enter as Non-Purchase Payment in Cash Book   page 130
    4 Cash Book
        2 Enter/Change Journals
            2 Enter/Change Cash Payments/Purchases
            (Use **1** – Current Bank A/C)

Enter New Product

Enter new Product   page 144
    5 Stock
        1 Products/Services
            1 Maintain Product/Service

Central

Customising the Company   page 100
    0 Central
        1 General Company Information
            1 Company Configuration

TASBooks Configuration   page 84
    0 Central
        1 General Company Information
            2 TASBooks Configuration

VAT 3 Report   page 150
    0 Central
        3 VAT Rates/Reporting
            3 VAT Return Manager

Nominal Ledger

Sales Ledger

Un-allocate/Delete Receipt   page 141
  2 Sales
    5 Receipts
      2 Unallocate/Delete Sales Ledger Receipts

Setting the Sales Ledger Date   page 156
  2 Sales
    9 End of Period Programs
      9 Change Sales Ledger Date

Purchase Ledger

Maintain Supplier Standing Data (New Supplier)   page 139
  3 Purchase
    1 Suppliers
      Maintain Suppliers

Supplier Account Enquiry   page 127
  3 Purchase
    1 Suppliers
      2 Supplier Account Enquiry

Editing/Deleting a Posting   page 120
  Recall Posting using **Posting No:**

Purchases/Cash Daybook Report   page 126
  3 Purchase
    4 Purchase Ledger Reports
      1 Print Purchase/Cash Daybooks

Aged Creditors Report   page 151
  3 Purchase
    4 Purchase Ledger Reports
      2 Print Aged Creditors Report

Un-allocate/Delete Payments   page 141
  3 Purchase
    5 Payments on Account
      2 Unallocate/Delete Purchase Ledger Payments

Setting the Ledger Date   page 156
  3 Purchase
    9 End of Period Programs
      9 Change Purchase Ledger Date

Cash Book

Cash Receipts (incl. Capital Investment)   page 131
    4 Cash Book
        2 Enter/Change Journals
            1 Enter/Change Cash Receipts/Sales

Print Cash Book Payments/Receipts   page 152
    4 Cash Book
        2 Reporting
            1 Print Cash Book Payments/Receipts
            (Select 1 – Current Bank A/C)

Petty Cash Book Payments Report   page 153
    4 Cash Book
        4 Reporting
            1 Print Cash Book Payments/Receipts
            (Select 2 – Petty Cash account)

Stock

Enter New Products and Services   page 144
    5 Stock
        1 Product/Services
            1 Maintain Product/Service

Edit Product and Services Details   page 144
    5 Stock
        1 Product/Services
            1 Maintain Product/Service
            (Edit **Product** details)

Print Products Details   page 148
    5 Stock
        3 Products/Services Reporting
        1 Print Products Details

Sales Orders

Enter Sales Order   page 106
    6 Sales Orders
        1 Sales Orders
            1 Enter/Change Sales Orders/Credit Notes

Editing/Deleting a Sales Order

page 106

    6 Sales Orders

        1 Sales Orders

            1 Enter/Change Sales Orders/Credit Notes

            (Type the **Order No.** required)

Sales Order Enquiry

page 109

    6 Sales Orders

        1 Sales Orders

            2 Sales Order Enquiry

Print and Post Sales Invoices and Credit Notes

page 108

    6 Sales Orders

        2 Print and Post

            5 Print Sales Invoices/Credit Notes

14 Exercises C-1, C-2, C-3 and C-4

Exercise C-1

Tasks C-1 through C-41 must be completed in order to carry out this exercise.

1 Enter any adjustments needed as a result of the Bank Reconciliation.

2 Change the ledger dates (Nominal, Sales, Purchases) to 28/02/##.

3 Create additional customer accounts for the customers listed on Source Documents page 22.

4 Create additional supplier accounts for the suppliers listed on Source Documents page 22.

5 Create additional nominal accounts from the details listed on Source Documents page 22.

6 Enter additional products from the details listed on Source Documents page 22.

7 Create invoices and credit notes from the details listed on page 23–24. (Remember to allocate the credit notes, and enter and allocate the receipt of the cash for the cash sale.)

8 Enter the information from Source Documents pages 37–58 into the appropriate accounts.

9 A direct debit of €1532.75 was made for salaries on 28/02/##. Write up this transaction in the appropriate daybook.

10 Cheque number 200207 was cashed on 28/02/## to restore the petty cash imprest to €100.00. Calculate the amount of this cheque and enter it in the appropriate daybook.

11 Produce the following printouts (these may be displayed on screen instead): (Compare your reports with the Daybooks, Ledgers and trial balance obtained from Exercise M-1.)

- Trial balance as at the last day of February ##
- Sales Daybook for February ##
- Purchase Daybook for February ##
- Cheque Payment report for February ##
- Petty Cash Payments for February ##
- Cheque Receipts for February ##
- A list of product details
- VAT 3 report

12 Perform a Bank Reconciliation using the bank statement on Source Documents page 59.

13 Extract the following from the VAT 3 report:
- The amount of VAT which would be payable or repayable to (or from) the Collector General for March ##. Write this figure on the VAT 3 report.

14 Back up the data files.

Exercise C-2

Exercise C-1 must be completed in order to carry out the following tasks.

1 Enter any adjustments needed as a result of the Bank Reconciliation.

2 Create additional customer accounts for the customers listed on Source Documents page 61.

3 Create additional supplier accounts for the suppliers listed on Source Documents page 61.

4 Create additional Nominal accounts from the details listed on Source Documents page 61.

5 Enter additional products from the details listed on Source Documents page 61.

6 Create invoices and credit notes from the details listed on Source Documents page 62.
(Remember to allocate the credit notes and enter and allocate the receipt of the cash for the cash sale.)

7 Enter the information from Source Documents pages 69–83 into the appropriate accounts.

8 Cheque number 200304 was sent to the Collector General on 12/03/## to pay the VAT for January and February. Calculate the amount of this cheque and enter it in the appropriate daybook.

9 Enter the following direct debit payments in the appropriate accounts:
- €345.00 was paid for rent on 28/03/##
- €1654.25 was made for salaries on 31/03/##

10 Cheque number 200305 was cashed on 31/03/## to restore the petty cash imprest to €100.00. Calculate the amount of this cheque and enter it in the appropriate daybook.

11 Produce the following printouts (these may be displayed on screen instead):
(Compare your reports with the Daybooks, Ledgers and trial balance obtained from the Manual Exercise.)
- Trial balance as at the last day of March ##
- Sales Daybook for March ##
- Purchase Daybook for March ##
- Cash/Cheque Payment Report for March ##
- Petty Cash Payments Report for March ##
- Cash/Cheque Receipts Report for March ##
- The Electrical Shop account for January, February and March
- Solon International account for January, February and March
- The Purchases Nominal account for March
- A list of product details
- VAT 3 report

12 Perform a Bank Reconciliation using the Bank Statement on Source Documents page 84.

13 Extract the following from the VAT 3 report:
- The amount of VAT which would be payable or repayable to (or from) the Collector General for March ##. Write this figure on the VAT 3 report.

14 Back up the data files.

Exercise C-3

The following company has been set up on your computer:
Gem Jewellers
Patrick's Street
Cork City
Co. Cork
Carry out each of the following tasks:

1 Create Customer accounts for the customers listed on Source Documents page 90.

2 Create Supplier accounts for the suppliers listed on Source Documents page 90.

3 Create Nominal accounts from the details listed on Source Documents page 91.

4 Enter Products from the details listed on Source Documents page 91.

5 The company commenced business on 01/01/## with capital of €25,000.00, depositing €24,800.00 in their current bank account and €200.00 in their Petty Cash account. Enter this information in the appropriate accounts.

6 Create sales invoices and credit notes from the details listed on Source Documents page 92.
(Remember to allocate the credit notes and enter and allocate the receipt of the cash for the cash sale.)

7 Enter the information from Source Documents pages 101–113 into the appropriate accounts.

8 Enter the following direct debit payments into the appropriate accounts:
   • Rent payment of €450.00 on 25/01/##
   • Salary payment of €1108.56 on 30/01/##

9 Cheque No. 215014 was cashed on 31/01/## to restore the petty cash imprest to €200.00. Determine the amount of this cheque and enter the transaction into the appropriate accounts.

10 Produce the following printouts:
   • Trial balance as at 31 January ##
   • Sales Daybook for January ##
   • Purchase Daybook for January ##
   • Cheque Payment report for January ##
   • Petty Cash Payments for January ##
   • Cheque Receipts for January ##
   • A list of product details
   • VAT 3 report

11 Perform a Bank Reconciliation using the Bank Statement on Source Documents page 114.

12 Extract the following from the VAT 3 report:
   • The amount of VAT which would be payable or repayable to (or from) the Collector General for January ##.

13 Back up the data files.

Exercise C-4

Exercise C-3 must be completed in order to carry out the following tasks:

1 Enter any adjustments needed as a result of the Bank Reconciliation.

2 Change the ledger dates (Nominal, Sales, Purchases) to 28/02/##.

3 Create additional customer accounts for the customers listed on Source Documents page 116.

4 Create additional supplier accounts for the suppliers listed on Source Documents page 116.

5 Create additional Nominal accounts from the details listed on Source Documents page 116.

6 Enter additional products from the details listed on Source Documents page 117.

7 Gem Jewellers, Patrick's Street, Cork, invested a further €8,000 in their business on 01/02/## which was deposited in their current bank account. Use the General Journal to record this transaction.

8 Create sales invoices and credit notes from the details listed on Source Documents pages 117–119.
(Remember to allocate the credit notes and enter and allocate the receipt of the cash for the cash sale.)

9 Enter the information from the Source Documents pages 120–168 into the appropriate accounts.

10 Enter the following direct debit payments into the appropriate accounts:
- Rent payment of €450.00 on 26/02/##
- Salary payment of €1317.84 on 28/02/##

11 Cheque No. 215205 was cashed on 28/02/## to restore the Petty Cash imprest to €200.00. Determine the amount of this cheque and enter the transaction into the appropriate accounts.

12 Produce the following printouts:
- Trial balance as at 28 February ##
- Sales Daybook for February ##
- Purchase Daybook for February ##
- Cheque Payment report for February ##
- Petty Cash Payments for February ##
- Cheque Receipts for February ##
- A list of product Details
- VAT 3 report

13 Perform a Bank Reconcilliation using the Bank Statement on Source Documents page 169.

14 Extract the following from the VAT 3 report:
- The amount of VAT which would be payable or repayable to (or from) the Collector General for January and February ##. Write this figure on the VAT 3 report.

15 Back up the data files.

PART 4

Sample Manual Project for Bookkeeping – Manual and Computerised Module

1 Sample Manual Project

Project

On completion of the project the candidate must return this brief, source documents, daybooks, ledgers and answer sheet(s).

Candidate name: _____ *Date:* _____

Company Profile

Business Name:	Computer Services

Address:

Unit 106
Renwood Park
Galway

Telephone:	091–556827

Fax:	091–556876

VAT Reg Number:	IE4568942F

- Computer Services is engaged in the sale and maintenance of computers. They purchase computers from a single source and peripherals from a different source.
- The company is registered for VAT.
- The company is engaged in both cash and credit sales.

Instructions to Candidates

Carry out each task in the order in which they are listed.

1 The company commenced business on 1 January 20## with capital of
   €60,000.00, depositing €59,800.00 in their current bank account and
   €200.00 in their Petty Cash account. **Enter** this information in the
   appropriate daybook.

2 From the source documents provided on Source Documents pages
   173–186, **write up** the following daybooks:
   • Sales/Sales Returns Daybook
   • Purchases/Purchases Returns Daybook
   • Bank Lodgement Book
   • Bank Payments Book
   • Petty Cash Book

3 **Write up** the following transaction in the appropriate daybook:
   • Rent payment of €650.00 on 29 January 20##

4 Cheque No. 300103 was cashed on 31 January 20## to restore the Petty
   Cash imprest (float) to €200.00. **Determine** the amount of this cheque
   and **enter** the transaction into the appropriate daybook.

5 **Post** the entries in the daybooks to the appropriate Ledger accounts.

6 **Extract** a trial balance as at 31 January.

7 **Perform** a Bank Reconciliation using the Bank Statement on Source
   Documents page 187.

8 **Extract** the required VAT details from the records and **complete** the VAT 3
   form.

2 Sample Solution

Manual Project Sample Solution

COMPANY NAME: COMPUTER SERVICES

Sales/Sales Returns Daybook   Month: Jan 20##

Date	Customer	F	Inv./Cr. Nt. Number	Total	Net Amount @ 21%	@ 12.5%	VAT Amount	Analysis Sales	Repairs
04/01/##	James Kenny	SL	100001	€5250.00	€4375.00	–	€875.00	€4375.00	–
06/01/##	Mary Byrne	SL	100002	€1192.50	€825.00	€180.00	€187.50	€825.00	€180.00
0801/##	Cash Sale	SL	100003	€1116.56	€825.00	€112.50	€179.06	€825.00	€112.50
10/01/##	Mary Byrne	SL	100004	€6540.00	€5450.00	–	€1090.00	€5450.00	–
12/01/##	James Kenny	SL	100005	(€2130.00)	(€1775.00)	–	(€355.00)	(€1775.00)	–
			Totals:	€11969.06	€9700.00	€292.50	€1976.56	€9700.00	€292.50
							NL	NL	NL

COMPANY NAME: COMPUTER SERVICES

Cash Receipts (Bank Lodgement) Book   Month: Jan 20##

Date	Details	Lodge No.	F	Bank	Cash Sales	Debtors	Other
08/01/##	Cash Sale	100	SL	€1116.56	€1116.56		
10/01/##	Mary Byrne (cheque no 300248)	101	SL	€1192.50		€1192.50	
11/01/##	James Kenny (cheque no 400125)	102	SL	€3000.00		€3000.00	
		Totals:		€5309.06	€1116.56	€4192.50	€0.00
				NL			

COMPANY NAME: COMPUTER SERVICES

Purchases/Purchases Returns Daybook   Month: Jan 20##

Date	Supplier	F	Inv./Cr.Nt. Number	Total	Goods for Resale Net@21%	Goods for Resale Net@12.5%	Goods N for R Net@21%	VAT Amnt	Purchases	Analysis Elec.	Analysis Tel.	Analysis Fix. & Fit.
03/01/##	Samala Inter.	PL	35781	€11700.00	€9750.00			€1950.00	€9750.00			
04/01/##	Computer Periph.	PL	3487	€600.00	€500.00			€100.00	€500.00			
13/01/##	Samala Inter.	PL	647	(€2340.00)	(€1950.00)			(€390.00)	(€1950.00)			
14/01/##	Modern Communic.	PL		€99.34			€82.78	€16.56			€82.78	
			Totals:	€10059.24	€8300.00	€0.00	€82.78	€1676.56	€8300.00	€0.00	€82.78	€0.00
				NL			NL	NL		NL		

COMPANY NAME: COMPUTER SERVICES

Cash (Bank) Payments Book   Month: Jan 20##

Date	Details	Cheque No	F	Total	Analysis Creditors	Analysis Salaries	Analysis Rent	Analysis Petty Cash	Analysis Other
26/01/##	Modern Communications	300101	PL	€99.34	€99.34				
26/01/##	Samala International	300102	PL	€9360.00	€9360.00				
29/01/##	Rent Payment		DD	€650.00			€650.00		
31/01/##	Restore Petty Cash Imprest	300103		€25.07				€25.07	
		Totals:		€10134.41	€9459.34	€0.00	€650.00	€25.07	€0.00
				NL			NL	NL	

COMPANY NAME: COMPUTER SERVICES

Petty Cash Book   Month: Jan 20##

Date	Expenditure	Voucher Number	Total	VAT	Analysis			
					Post	Stationery	Cleaning	Misc. Exp.
05/01/##	Stamps	1	€3.50		€3.50			
08/01/##	Blank CDs	2	€6.24	€1.04				€5.20
15/01/##	Window Cleaning	3	€10.13	€1.13			€9.00	
18/01/##	Envelopes	4	€5.20			€5.20		
		Totals:	€25.12	€2.22	€3.50	€5.20	€9.00	€5.20
			NL	NL	NL	NL	NL	NL

COMPANY NAME: COMPUTER SERVICES

General Journal   Month: Jan 20##

Date	Details	F	Debit	Credit
01/01/##	Bank Current A/C	NL	€59,800.00	
01/01/##	Petty Cash	NL	€200.00	
01/01/##	Capital	NL		€60,000.00
	(Capital investment lodged)			
	Totals:		€60,000.00	€60,000.00

COMPANY NAME: COMPUTER SERVICES

Sales (Debtors') Ledger   Debtor (Customer): James Kenny

Date	Details	F	Dr	Cr	Bal
04/01/##	Sales (Invoice 1001)	SB	€5250.00		€5250.00
11/01/##	Receipt (cheque no 400125)	CRB		€3000.00	€2520.00
12/01/##	Credit (Credit Note 1005)	SB		€2130.00	€120.00

Sales (Debtors') Ledger   Debtor (Customer): Mary Byrne

Date	Details	F	Dr	Cr	Bal
06/01/##	Sales (Invoice 1002)	SB	€1192.50		€1192.50
10/01/##	Sales (Invoice 1004)	SB	€6540.00		€7732.50
10/01/##	Receipt (cheque no 300248)	CRB		€1192.50	€6540.00

Sales (Debtors') Ledger   Debtor (Customer): Cash Sales

Date	Details	F	Dr	Cr	Bal
08/01/##	Sales (Invoice 1003)	SB	€1116.56		€1116.56
08/01/##	Receipt (Cash)	CRB		€1116.56	€0.00

COMPANY NAME: COMPUTER SERVICES

Purchases (Creditors') Ledger   Creditor (Supplier): Samala Intern.

Date	Details	F	Dr	Cr	Bal
03/01/##	Purchases (Invoice 35781)	PB		€11700.00	€11700.00
13/01/##	Returns (credit note no 647)	PB	€2340.00		€9360.00
26/##/##	Payment (cheque no 300102)	CPB	€9360.00	€0.00	

Purchases (Creditors') Ledger   Creditor (Supplier): Computer Periph.

Date	Details	F	Dr	Cr	Bal
04/01/##	Purchases (Invoice 3487)	PB		€600.00	€600.00

Purchases (Creditors') Ledger   Creditor (Supplier): Modern Commun.

Date	Details	F	Dr	Cr	Bal
14/01/##	Telephone Bill (Invoice)	PB		€99.34	€99.34
26/01/##	Payment (cheque no 300101)	CPB	€99.34		€0.00

COMPANY NAME: COMPUTER SERVICES

Nominal (General) Ledger — Nominal Account: Sales

Date	Details	F	Dr	Cr	Bal
31/01/##	Sales (Jan ##)	SB		€9700.00	€9700.00

Nominal (General) Ledger — Nominal Account: Repairs

Date	Details	F	Dr	Cr	Bal
31/01/##	Repairs (Jan ##)	SB		€292.50	€292.50

Nominal (General) Ledger — Nominal Account: Purchases

Date	Details	F	Dr	Cr	Bal
31/01/##	Purchases (Jan ##)	PB	€8300.00		€8300.00

Nominal (General) Ledger — Nominal Account: Telephone

Date	Details	F	Dr	Cr	Bal
31/01/##	Telephone (Jan ##)	PB	€82.78		€82.78

Nominal (General) Ledger — Nominal Account: Rent

Date	Details	F	Dr	Cr	Bal
31/01/##	Rent (Jan ##)	CPB	€650.00		€650.00

COMPANY NAME: COMPUTER SERVICES

Nominal (General) Ledger Nominal Account: Post

Date	Details	F	Dr	Cr	Bal
31/01/##	Post (Jan ##)	PCB	€3.50		€3.50

Nominal (General) Ledger Nominal Account: Stationery

Date	Details	F	Dr	Cr	Bal
31/01/##	Stationery (Jan ##)	PCB	€5.20		€5.20

Nominal (General) Ledger Nominal Account: Cleaning

Date	Details	F	Dr	Cr	Bal
31/01/##	Cleaning (Jan ##)	PCB	€9.00		€9.00

Nominal (General) Ledger Nominal Account: Miscellaneous Expenses

Date	Details	F	Dr	Cr	Bal
31/01/##	Misc. Exp. (Jan ##)	PCB	€5.20		€5.20

Nominal (General) Ledger Nominal Account: Bank Current A/C

Date	Details	F	Dr	Cr	Bal
01/01/##	Capital Investment	GJ	€59,800.00		€59,800.00
31/01/##	Bank Lodgements (Jan ##)	CRB	€5,309.06		€65109.06
31/01/##	Cash Payments (Jan ##)	CPB		€10134.41	€54974.65

COMPANY NAME: COMPUTER SERVICES

Nominal (General) Ledger   Nominal Account: Petty Cash

Date	Details	F	Dr	Cr	Bal
01/01/##	Opening Balance	GJ	€200.00		€200.00
31/01/##	Total Payments (Jan ##)	PCB		€25.07	€174.93
31/01/##	Restore Imprest	BPB	€25.07		€200.00

Nominal (General) Ledger   Nominal Account: VAT Payable

Date	Details	F	Dr	Cr	Bal
31/01/##	VAT on Sales (Jan ##)	SDB		€1976.56	€1976.56
31/01/##	VAT on Purchases (Jan ##)	PDB	€1676.56		€300.00
31/01/##	VAT on Petty Cash Purchases (Jan ##)	PCB		€2.17	€297.83

Nominal (General) Ledger   Nominal Account: Capital

Date	Details	F	Dr	Cr	Bal
01/01/##	Capital Investment	GJ		€60,000.00	€60,000.00

COMPUTER SERVICES

TRIAL BALANCE AS AT 31/01/##

	Debit	Credit
Debit Credit Sales		€9,700.00
Repairs		€292.50
Purchases	€8,300.00	
Rent	€650.00	
Telephone	€82.78	
Post	€3.50	
Stationery	€5.20	
Cleaning	€ 9.00	
Miscellaneous Expenses	€5.20	
Debtors	€6,660.00	
Bank Current Account	€54,974.65	
Petty Cash	€200.00	
Creditors		€600.00
VAT Payable		€297.83
Capital		€60,000.00
	€70,890.33	€70,890.33

COMPUTER SERVICES

BANK RECONCILIATION

Balance as per bank statement	€ 54,971.17
Adjustments: Add deposits not shown on bank statement	+ € 0.00
Subtract cheques issued but not shown on bank statement	- € 25.07
Subtract any payments recorded in own accounts but not shown on bank statement (e.g. DD or SO)	- € 0.00
Adjusted Bank Balance	€ 54,946.10

Balance as per bank Nominal ledger	€ 54,974.65
Adjustments:	
Add interest earned	+ € 0.00
Subtract bank charges	– € 28.55
Add/Subtract any errors in Nominal bank account	+ € 0.00
Adjusted Bank Nominal Ledger	€ 54,946.10

In all correspondence please Quote

Registration No: IE 75R46R2P

Notice No: 06334829-00040P

67839 151968 67521 1511481 000312VAT3EP

Collector-Generals
Sarsfield House
Francis Street
Limerick
District 358   Unit 257

VAT Period:

01 Jan 20##

to

31 Jan 20##

Payment due by:

15 Feb 20##

J.P. Murphy Electric
Main Street
Naas
Co Kildare

Enquiries: 1890 263070

VAT 3 RETURN

Please complete and sign the return below. The return should then be detached and forwarded (with payment or debit instructions, if liability arises) in the prepaid envelope enclosed, to arrive no later than the due date as shown above. **Guidelines on the correct completion of the return are shown overleaf.**

IMPORTANCE OF PROMPT PAYMENTS
 • Make sure that you allow sufficient time - at least three working days - for your payment to reach the Collector-General.
 • Late payment of tax may incur an interest charge.
 • Failure to pay a tax liability, or to pay on time, can result in enforced collection through the Sheriff, Court proceedings or Attachment.
Enforcement gives rise to costs in addition to any interest charged.

METHOD OF PAYMENT
Single Debit Authority: If you want your payment to be debited directly from your bank account, complete the bank details on the left of the return below, ensuring that the amount of the payment you wish to make is entered in the Debit Amount box.
Please note that the account must be in a bank within the Republic of Ireland and must be a current account.
 • Simply provide your bank details and the amount you wish to have debited from your account.
 • Forward the completed return to the Collector-General at the address above.
 • A once-off deduction will be taken from your account and credited against your tax liability as specified on the return below.
 • The once-off deduction will not be taken from your account in advance of the due date for the taxable period in question.
Cheque: All cheques should be made payable to the Collector-General and forwarded to the address above. Do not enclose cash.
Revenue On-Line Service (ROS): You can make this return and pay your VAT on-line using ROS. For details visit the Revenue website at www.revenue.ie or Phone 1890 20 11 06.
Direct Debit: For information on how to pay VAT by monthly Direct Debit, please contact the Helpline at 1890 20 30 70.

METHOD OF REPAYMENT
Any repayment due will be credited to your bank/building society account. Account details are only required *if* this return is a repayment (T4 line completed) *and* you have not previously advised Revenue of the account details *or* you wish to amend the account details to which previous repayments were credited.

Please print one figure only in each space using a black ball-point pen. **€: Enter whole Euro only - do not enter cent.**
Do not write NIL on any line. Photocopies of this form are not acceptable.

Revenue

| ↓ VAT3 RETURN (and PAYSLIP) | Please complete below, detach and return ↓ |

Bank Details - to be supplied if :
⇒ Payment is being made by Single Debit Authority
  (do not complete this authority if you are paying by cheque), or
⇒ A repayment is being sought (see Method of Repayment above).

Branch Sort Code

Account Number

Single Debit Authority

Debit Amount   .00

Please debit my account with the amount specified.

	VAT on Sales			
T1		1 8 2 4	.00
	VAT on Purchases			
T2		1 4 3 9	.00
	Excess of T1 over T2 (Payable)			
T3		3 8 5	.00
	or Excess of T2 over T1 (Repayable)			
T4			.00
	Amount of Payment			
			.00

Value of Goods Sent to other EU Countries

E1   .00

Value of Goods Received from other EU Countries

E2   .00

I declare that this is a correct return of Value Added Tax for the period specified.

Signed:- _____ Date:- _____

VAT3

B

3 Sample Project Marking Scheme

Manual Project

4 Sales Invoices   [Sales/Sales Returns Daybook]   12 marks
    Mark per invoice entered
        ½ mark – date
        ½ mark – detail
        ½ mark – total inclusive
        ½ mark – exclusive
        ½ mark – VAT
        ½ mark – analysis

3 Purchases Invoices   [Purchases/Purchases Returns Daybook]   9 marks
    Mark per invoice entered
        ½ mark – date
        ½ mark – detail
        ½ mark – total inclusive
        ½ mark – exclusive
        ½ mark – VAT
        ½ mark – analysis

2 Returns   [Sales/Sales Returns and Purchases/   6 marks
                      Purchases Returns Book]
    Mark per entry in Returns Book
        ½ mark – date
        ½ mark – detail
        ½ mark – total inclusive
        ½ mark – exclusive
        ½ mark – VAT
        ½ mark – analysis

2 Receipts   [Cash Receipts (Bank Lodgement) Book]   4 marks

     Mark per receipt

          ½ mark – date
          ½ mark – detail
          ½ mark – bank
          ½ mark – analysis

4 Payments   [Cash (Bank) Payments Book]   8 marks

     Mark per payment

          ½ mark – date
          ½ mark – detail
          ½ mark – total
          ½ mark – analysis

3 Petty Cash Payments [Petty Cash Book]   9 marks

     Mark per item entered in Petty Cash Book

          ½ mark – date
          ½ mark – detail
          1 mark – amount
          1 mark – analysis

2 Debtors   [Sales (Debtors') Ledger]   6 marks

     Debtor James Kenny

          1 mark – sales amount
          1 mark – bank amount
          1 mark – balance amount

     Debtor Mary Byrne

          ½ mark – 1st sale
          ½ mark – 2nd sale
          ½ mark – returns
          ½ mark – bank
          1 mark – balance amount

3 Creditors   [Purchases (Creditors') Ledger]   6 marks

     Samala International

          ½ mark – 1st purchase
          ½ mark – 2nd
          ½ mark – bank
          ½ mark – returns
          1 mark – balance/adjusting balance

     Computer Peripherals

          ½ mark – purchase
          ½ mark – bank
          ½ mark – balance amount

Modern Communications
½ mark – purchase
½ mark – bank
½ mark – balance amount

10 Nominal Accounts	[Nominal (General) Ledger]	24 marks
VAT A/C = 4 marks	[1 mark per transaction or opening balance. 1 mark for balance]	
Bank A/C = 4 marks	[1 mark per transaction or opening balance. 1 mark for balance]	

Other Accounts = 2 marks each

Opening Balance = 1 and transaction = 1
OR
Opening Balance = 0 and transaction = 2

Trial Balance	[Trial Balance]	4 marks

1 mark – list of accounts
1 mark – debit figures
1 mark – credit figures
1 mark – total figures

Deduct ½ mark for each item transferred incorrectly from ledgers to maximum of 4 marks.

Do not deduct for same error twice, i.e. if account is incorrect in ledger, but is transferred to trial balance correctly, award the mark.

Bank Reconciliation   6 marks

Bank Reconciliation completed accurately
(Deduct 1 mark for each incorrect figure.)

VAT Form	[VAT 3 Form]	6 marks

2 mark – T1
2 mark – T2
2 mark – T3

PART 5

Sample Computerised Examination for Bookkeeping – Manual and Computerised Module

1 Sample Computerised Examination

Computerised Examination

On completion of the examination the candidate must return the
examination paper, source documents and printouts.

Candidate name: _____ Date:_____

Company Profile

Business Name:

Computer Services

Address:

Unit 106
Renwood Park
Galway

Telephone:

091–556827

Fax:

091–556876

VAT Reg Number:

IE4568942F

- Computer services are engaged in the sale and maintenance of computers. They purchase computers from a single source and peripherals from a different source.
- The company is registered for VAT.
- The company is engaged in both cash and credit sales.
- The required default accounts for the Sales Ledger, Purchase Ledger, Nominal Ledger and VAT codes have been created for the above company.

Instructions to Candidates

Carry out each task in the order in which they are listed.

1   **Create Customer Accounts** as follows:

Name	Code	Address
James Kenny	K001	Main Street Ballinasloe Co. Galway
Mary Byrne	B001	Willowbank Salthill Co. Galway
Cash Sales	C001	Cash Sales

2   **Create Supplier Accounts** as follows:

Name	Code	Address
Samala International	S101	Unit 12 Sunshine Industrial Est. Crumlin Road Dublin 12 Tel: 01-868 2578
Computer Peripherals	C101	Unit 118 Kenwood Place Dublin 8 Tel: 01-646 4587
Modern Communications	M101	City West Park Naas Road Co. Dublin Tel: 01-535 6274

3 **Create Nominal Accounts** as follows:

Number	Description	Type	Group	Dr or Cr
• 1100	Repairs Income	Income	Income	Cr
• 3100	Rent	Expense	Expense	Dr
• 3200	Electricity	Expense	Expense	Dr
• 3300	Telephone	Expense	Expense	Dr
• 3400	Post	Expense	Expense	Dr
• 3500	Stationery	Expense	Expense	Dr
• 3600	Cleaning	Expense	Expense	Dr
• 3700	Miscellaneous Expenses	Expense	Expense	Dr
• 9000	Capital	Owner Eq	Owner Eq	Cr

4 **Enter** the following product details:

PRODUCT STOCK	CODE	VAT RATE	SELLING PRICE
Computer	C111	20%	€825.00
Printer	P101	20%	€125.00
Repairs	R100	12.5%	€22.50

5 The company commenced business on 1 January 20## with capital of €60,000.00, depositing €59,800.00 in their current bank account and €200.00 in their Petty Cash account. Enter this information in the appropriate accounts.

6 **Create** Sales Invoices and Credit Note(s) from the details shown below. **Print** and **Post** each of these documents.

Invoices

DATE	CUSTOMER	PRODUCT CODE	QTY.
04/01/##	James Kenny	C111	5
		P101	2
06/01/##	Mary Byrne	C111	1
		R100	8
08/01/##	Cash Sale	R100	5
	(Lodgement Slip No.: 100)	C111	1
10/01/##	Mary Byrne	C111	6
		P101	4

Credit Note

DATE	CUSTOMER	PRODUCT CODE	QTY.
12/01/##	James Kenny	C111	2
	P101	1	

7 **Enter** the information supplied by the Source Documents pages 178–186 into the appropriate accounts.

8 **Enter** the following Direct Debit payment into the appropriate accounts:

- Rent payment of €650.00 on 29 January 20##

9 Cheque No. 300103 was cashed on 31 January 20## to restore the Petty Cash imprest (float) to €200.00. **Determine** the amount of this cheque and **enter** the transaction into the appropriate accounts.

10 **Produce** the following printouts. Printing may be performed after the examination time but no alterations may be made to the files.

- All Invoices and Credit Notes
- Trial balance as at 31 January 20##
- Sales Daybook for January 20##
- Purchase Daybook for January 20##
- Cheque Payment report for January 20##
- Petty Cash Payments for January 20##
- Cheque Receipts for January 20##
- Product price list
- VAT 3 report

11 **Extract** the following from the VAT 3 report:

- The amount of VAT which would be payable or repayable to (or from) the Collector General for January 20##. Enter this figure on the VAT 3 report form.

12 **Back up** the data files.

2 Sample Solution

Computerised Examination Sample Solution

Computer Services					Invoice No:		100001
Unit 106					Invoice Date / Tax Point:		12/01/##
Renwood Park					Page:		1
Galway							
Co. Galway							
N/A							
Ireland							
Tel: 091-556827, Fax: 091-556876					VAT Number:		IE-4568942F

Invoice to:
James Kenny
Main Street
Ballinasloe
Co. Galway

Deliver to:
James Kenny
Main Street
Ballinasloe
Co. Galway

Your Ref: **Desc:** Sales Order **Customer Code:** K001
Our Ref: 200001 **Order Date:** 04/01/##

Description	V	Ord Qty	B/O Qty	Ship Qty	Price	Disc %	Total
Computer	1	5.00	0.00	5.00	825.00	0.00	4,125.00
Printer	1	2.00	0.00	2.00	125.00	0.00	250.00

VAT Rate	Net Amt	VAT Amt		NET:	4,375.00
1 20.00%	4,375.00	857.00		VAT:	875.00
				TOTAL:	5,250.00

Computer Services				Invoice No:		100002	

Computer Services
Unit 106
Renwood Park
Galway
Co. Galway
N/A
Ireland
Tel: 091-556827, Fax: 091-556876

Invoice No: 100002
Invoice Date / Tax Point: 12/01/##
Page: 1

VAT Number: IE-4568942F

Invoice to:
Mary Byrne
Willowbank
Salthill
Co. Galway

Deliver to:
Mary Byrne
Willowbank
Salthill
Co. Galway

Your Ref: **Desc:** Sales Order   Customer Code: B001
Our Ref: 200002   Order Date: 06/01/2012

Description	V	Ord Qty	B/O Qty	Ship Qty	Price	Disc %	Total
Computer	1	1.00	0.00	1.00	825.00	0.00	825.00
Repairs	2	8.00	0.00	8.00	22.50	0.00	180.00

VAT Rate	Net Amt	VAT Amt			
1 20.00%	825.00	165.00		**NET:**	1,005.00
1 12.50%	180.00	22.50		**VAT:**	187.50
				TOTAL:	1,192.50

Computer Services		Invoice No:	100003
Unit 106		Invoice Date / Tax Point:	12/01/2012
Renwood Park		Page:	1
Galway			
Co. Galway			
N/A			
Ireland			
Tel: 091-556827, Fax: 091-556876		VAT Number:	IE-4568942F

Invoice to: **Deliver to:**
Cash Sale   Cash Sale
Cash Sale   Cash Sale
Cash Sale   Cash Sale

Your Ref: **Desc:** Sales Order   **Customer Code:** C001
Our Ref: 200003   **Order Date:** 08/01/2012

Description	V	Ord Qty	B/O Qty	Ship Qty	Price	Disc %	Total
Repairs	2	5.00	0.00	5.00	22.50	0.00	112.50
Computer	1	1.00	0.00	1.00	825.00	0.00	825.00

VAT Rate	Net Amt	VAT Amt			NET:	936.50
1 20.00%	825.00	165.00			VAT:	179.06
2 12.50%	112.50	14.06			TOTAL:	1,116.56

Computer Services		Invoice No:	100004
Unit 106		Invoice Date / Tax Point:	12/01/2012
Renwood Park		Page:	1
Galway			
Co. Galway			
N/A			
Ireland			
Tel: 091-556827, Fax: 091-556876		VAT Number:	IE-4568942F

Invoice to:	Deliver to:
Mary Byrne	Mary Byrne
Willowbank	Willowbank
Salthill	Salthill
Co. Galway	Co. Galway

| Your Ref: | Desc: Sales Order | Customer Code: B001 |
| Our Ref: 200004 | | Order Date: 10/01/2012 |

Description	V	Ord Qty	B/O Qty	Ship Qty	Price	Disc %	Total
Computer	1	6.00	0.00	6.00	825.00	0.00	4,950.00
Repairs	2	4.00	0.00	4.00	125.00	0.00	500.00

VAT Rate	Net Amt	VAT Amt			
1 20.00%	5,450.00	1,090.00	NET:	5,450.00
			VAT:	1,090.00
			TOTAL:	6,540.00

Computer Services		Invoice No:	100005
Unit 106	Invoice Date / Tax Point:		12/01/#2012
Renwood Park		Page:	1
Galway			
Co. Galway			
N/A			
Ireland			
Tel: 091-556827, Fax: 091-556876		VAT Number:	IE-4568942F

Invoice to:
James Kenny
Main Street
Ballinasloe
Co. Galway

Deliver to:
James Kenny
Main Street
Ballinasloe
Co. Galway

Your Ref: **Desc:** Sales Order   **Customer Code:** K001
Our Ref: 200005   **Order Date:**   12/01/2012

Description	V	Ord Qty	B/O Qty	Ship Qty	Price	Disc %	Total
Computer	1	2.00	0.00	2.00	825.00	0.00	1,650.00
Printer	1	1.00	0.00	1.00	125.00	0.00	125.00

VAT Rate	Net Amt	VAT Amt			
1 20.00%	1,775.00	355.00		**NET:**	1,775.00
				VAT:	355.00
				TOTAL:	2,130.00

Starting Period: 01–01/01/2012　　　Computer Services　　　12/01/2012
Ending Period: 01–31/01/2012　　　Trial Balance – Current Year　　　3:29 p.m.

Acc	Dept	Description	Group	Period Debit	Period Credit	YTD Debit	YTD Credit
1000	100	Sales	INCOME		9,700.00		
1100	100	Repairs Income	INCOME		292.50		
2000	100	Purchases	EXPENSE	8,300.00		8,300.00	
3100	100	Rent	EXPENSE	650.00		650.00	
3300	100	Telephone	EXPENSE	82.78		82.78	
3400	100	Post	EXPENSE	3.50		3.50	
3500	100	Stationery	EXPENSE	5.20		5.20	
3600	100	Cleaning	EXPENSE	9.00		9.00	
3700	100	Miscellaneous Expenses	EXPENSE	5.20		5.20	
7000	100	Debtors	ASSET	6,660.00		6,660.00	
7200	100	Current Bank Account	ASSET	54,974.65		54,974.65	
7300	100	Petty Cash	ASSET	200.00		200.00	
8000	100	Creditors	LIABILITY		600.00		600.00
8100	100	VAT Payable	LIABILITY		297.83		297.83
9000	100	Capital	OWNER EQ		60,000.00		60,000.00
				70,890.33	70,890.33	70,890.33	70,890.33

Start: 01/01/2012   Computer Services   12/01/2012

End: 31/01/2012   (1) Sales Daybook   3:29 p.m.

Post	Pst Date	Cust Code	Inv No	Inv Date	T	Description	Net Amount	VAT Amount	Tot Amount	Project
100003	12/01/2012	K001	100001	12/01/2012	I	Sales Order	4,375.00	875.00	5,250.00	
100004	12/01/2012	B001	100002	12/01/2012	I	Sales Order	1,005.00	187.50	1,192.50	
100005	12/01/2012	C001	100003	12/01/2012	I	Sales Order	937.50	179.06	1,116.56	
100006	12/01/2012	B001	100004	12/01/2012	I	Sales Order	5,450.00	1,090.00	6,540.00	
100007	12/01/2012	K001	100005	12/01/2012	N	Credit Order	-1,775.00	-355.00	-2,130.00	
				Total Sales Invoices:			11,767.50	2,331.56	14,099.06	
				Total Credit Notes:			-1,775.00	-355.00	-2,130.00	
				Total Net Sales			9,992.50	1,976.56	11,969.06	
				Total Debit Journals/Refunds:			0.00	0.00	0.00	
				Total Credit Journals			0.00	0.00	0.00	
				Total Debit Interest			0.00	0.00	0.00	
				Total Credit Interst			0.00	0.00	0.00	
				Total Journals:			0.00	0.00	0.00	
				Grand Total:			9,992.50	1,976.56	11,969.06	

| Start: 01/01/2012 | | | | Computer Services | | | | | 12/01/2012 | |
| End: 31/01/2012 | | | | (1) Purchase Daybook | | | | | 3:29 p.m. | |

Post	Pst Date	Cust Code	Inv No	Inv Date	T	Description	Net Amount	VAT Amount	Tot Amount	Project
100008	01/01/2012	S101	3571	03/01/2012	I	Purchase Invoice	9,750.00	1,950.00	11,700.00	
100009	01/01/2012	C101	3487	04/01/2012	I	Purchase Invoice	500.00	100.00	600.00	
100015	31/01/2012	S101	647	13/01/2012	N	Credit Note	-1,950.00	-390.00	-2,340.00	
100016	31/01/2012	M101		14/01/2012	I	Telephone Bill	82.78	16.56	99.34	
						Total Purchase Invoices:	10,332.78	2,066.56	12,399.34	
						Total Credit Notes:	-1,950.00	-390.00	-2,340.00	
						Total Net Purchase:	8,382.78	1,676.56	10,059.34	
						Total Debit Journals/Refunds:	0.00	0.00	0.00	
						Total Credit Journals	0.00	0.00	0.00	
						Total Journals:	0.00	0.00	0.00	
						Grand Total:	8,382.76	1,676.56	10,059.34	

| Start: 01/01/2012 | | Computer Services | | | | | | | | 12/01/2012 |
| End: 31/01/2012 | | Payments Sorted by Date for Bank 1 – Current Account | | | | | | | | 3:30 p.m. |

Posting	Date	Code	Source	Inv Date	Description	Ref	Rec	Curr	Curr Amt	Total
100021	29/01/2012		CB DD	03/01/2012	Rent Payment	DD	N			650.00
100019	31/01/2012	M101	PL 300101	04/01/2012	PL Payment	300101	N			99.34
100020	31/01/2012	S101	PL 300102	13/01/2012	PL Payment	300102	N			9360.00
100022	31/01/2012		CB 300103	14/01/2012	Restore Petty Cash	300103	N			25.07
					Total Cash Payment:					10,134.41

Start: 01/01/2012   Computer Services   12/01/2012

End: 31/01/2012   Payments Sorted by Date for Bank 2-Current Account   3:30 p.m.

Posting	Date	Code	Source	Description	Ref	Rec	Curr	Curr Amt	Total
100010	05/01/2012		CB 1	Stamps	1	Y			3.50
100011	08/01/2012		CB 2	Blank CDs	2	Y			6.24
100017	15/01/2012		CB 3	Window Cleaning	3	Y			10.13
100018	18/01/2012		CB 4	Envelopes	4	Y			5.20
				Total Cash Payment:				25.07	

Start: 01/01/2012   Computer Services   12/01/2012

End: 31/01/2012   Cash Receipts Sorted by Date for Bank 1-Current Account   3:30 p.m.

Posting	Date	Code	Source	Description	Ref	Rec	Curr	Curr Amt	Total
100001	01/01/2012		CB START	Capital Lodged	START	N			59,800.00
100012	31/01/2012	C001	SL Cash	Cash Sale	100	N			1,116.56
100013	31/01/2012	B001	SL 300248	SL Receipt	101	N			1,192.50
100014	31/01/2012	K001	SL 400125	SL Receipt	102	N			3,000.00
				Total Cash Receipts:					65,109.06

Start: C111   Computer Services   12/01/2012

End: R100   Product Price List   3:32 p.m.

Code	Description	Un it Desc	VAT %	Cost	Retail	Retail (Ex VAT)	Trade	Wholesale
C111	Computer	Each	20.00%	0.00	990.00	825.00	0.00	0.00
P101	Printer	Each	20.00%	0.00	150.00	125.00	0.00	0.00
R100	Repairs	Each	12.50%	0.00	25.31	22.50	0.00	0.00

| Start Date: 01/01/2012 Computer Services | | 12/012/2012 |
| End Date: 29/02/2012 VAT 3 Report | | 3:33 p.m. |

Description	Box	Amount
Computer Services VAT Reg No: IE-4568942F		
Non-EC Services and Reverse Charge VAT Due:	T0	NIL
VAT charged by you on supplies of goods and services:	T1A	1,976
VAT due on intra-EU acquisitions:	T1B	NIL
TOTAL:	T1	1,976
Non-EC Services and Reverse Charge VAT Recovered:	T0	NIL
VAT on Stocks for resale:	T2A	1,660
VAT on other deductible goods and services:	T2B	18
TOTAL:	T2	1,678
Goods and Services Supplied & Intra-EU Acquisitions and imported parcels:	T1	1,976
VAT on Deductible Purchases, Intra-EU Acquisitions and Imports:	T2	1,678
Net Payable (Excess of T1 over T2):	T3	297
Net Payable (Excess of T2 over T1):	T4	NIL
Total goods to other EU countries:	E1	NIL
Total goods from other EU countries:	E2	NIL
Notes: This is a preview only. Figures are subject to change.		
VAT Payable to Collector General = €297		

3 Sample Examination Marking Scheme

Computerised Examination

Set-up

- Ledger accounts opened accurately   **12 marks**
  - 3 sales (customers and cash)   (4 marks)
  - 3 purchase (suppliers)   (4 marks)
  - 6 nominal   (4 marks)
- Stock details entered accurately
  - 3 stock items   (4 marks)   **4 marks**
- Opening balances entered accurately
  - Capital, bank balance, petty cash   (4 marks)   **4 marks**

Processing

- Transactions
  - 5 sales
  - 4 purchase
  - 3 receipts
  - 3 petty cash purchases
  - 4 payments   (19 transactions @ 2.5 marks)   **47.5 marks**
- Petty cash imprest restored accurately   **2.5 marks**

Printing

- documents and reports printed accurately   **10 marks**

Analysis

- Report interpreted accurately   **10 marks**
  - e.g. VAT report figures interpreted

Security

- Data files backed up accurately   **10 marks**